Bird Songs Don't Lie

Writings from the Rez

Gordon Lee Johnson

Foreword by Deborah A. Miranda

Heyday, Berkeley, California

The columns in this book originally appeared in the *Press-Enterprise*, sometimes in slightly different form. "Indian Love," "One Hundred White Women," and "A Rez Take on Mission Food" originally appeared in *News from Native California*.

Library of Congress Cataloging-in-Publication Data is available.

Cover Photo: Patricia Ware
Cover and Interior Design/Typesetting: Ashley Ingram

Orders, inquiries, and correspondence should be addressed to:
Heyday
P.O. Box 9145, Berkeley, CA 94709
(510) 549-3564
www.heydaybooks.com

Printed in Dexter, Michigan, by Thomson-Shore

10 9 8 7 6 5 4 3 2 1

To my children—Tyra, Missy, Brandon, and Jared—
in whose eyes I see myself a better man.

A shout-out to Matthew Goodman, a Vermont College mentor,
who with patience and skill unlocked secrets to the craft of fiction.
And to N. Scott Momaday, who made me want to write.

CONTENTS

FOREWORD

Although born at UCLA Hospital and raised for the first five years of my life in Los Angeles, I have lived most of my life far away from California. When I come home for a visit I see it with different eyes from those who have never left. Everything is new to me, and, at the same time, I remember and know every detail.

There should be a word for that, the way déjà vu means you feel like something has already happened even though you know it hasn't. Déjà vu is not it, not what I feel when I step out onto California land. This is, perhaps, more of a bone and blood memory: the air, minerals, water, scents, pollen, light, angle of the sun and stars that my body remembers, that some deep part of my brain remembers.

Usually this is triggered simply by being in California: feeling the thunder of surf on a flat sweep of beach, stepping over the rampant roots of huge fig trees bursting through slabs of sidewalk, or smelling eucalyptus on the evening air, running my hand along the ancient spears of agave or sitting beneath the shameless purple blossoms of jacaranda.

A few years ago in Westwood, I stepped on board a bus—and suddenly stepped back into my four-year-old body, going up those black steps, my hand in my mother's hand, sitting next to the window looking out at hot sidewalks and palm trees along the way. I had never remembered taking a bus with my mother in Los Angeles, yet now I felt as if I'd never been without that memory. It was as much a part of me as the color of my hair.

Science tells us that our bodies carry oxygen atoms from the water we drank as children; these isotopes are stored in our teeth. (Most teeth are formed either before birth or during childhood.) Therefore, analysis of our teeth tells the story of where we are from—we carry traces of our first home inside us, wherever we go. I've often wondered if this is the cause of the almost magnetic attraction I feel toward the landscapes of Southern California—the pull of my origins toward home. My experiences in California as a middle-aged woman are constantly doubled with memories of being a child there—sensory memories, emotional memories that shadow my every move. In some ways, it feels like walking simultaneously on two timelines; my two bodies—one three or four years old, one fifty-something—connected suddenly by the geographic location and my history with it.

Reading Gordon Lee Johnson's *Bird Songs Don't Lie* does the same thing to me. The stories within this collection—both memoir and fiction—pull on all my senses, spiral me through time: flashes of red chili sauce, cast-iron pans, fiesta, abalone shell, sage, old cars that won't die or die too soon, the familiar weight of adobe, the voices of aunties, the omnipresent Church, priest, death, hope. Gordon's rich memories intertwine with a world I remember, a world I have come back to time and time again, apprenticing myself to my elders, my relatives, and the land, in an effort to earn my place.

And yet, because Gordon has lived in California most of his life, his stories also fill in the empty spaces where my own memories are absent. His characters speak in honest, sometimes pain-filled voices about the complexities of contemporary life on a California rez, of living in the shadow of missionization, colonization, genocide, and all the ways those histories haunt us.

Perhaps what I appreciate most about the personal essays is the thoughtfulness of Gordon's observations about the ways tribal culture has endured, adapted, grown around obstacles, and sometimes faded, only to sprout up in some unexpected place.

"Luiseño Initiation" is one such moment: "I was born too late for an initiation ceremony," Gordon writes a little sadly, outlining the meticulous process that once involved hours, if not days, of preparation, deprivation, and the use of certain plants that shall not be named. He notes that "at the heart of the initiation ceremony was the lecture on how to conduct oneself in the right way."

Without missing a beat, he recaps the lecture as he's read about it in notes by a self-taught ethnologist from the 1890s, puts the advice into a language and context that makes sense for someone caught up in the complications of post-missionized reality. Reviewing these teachings, Gordon writes, "I take another sip of Negra Modelo, and I'm heartened." I love this line, the deceptive simplicity it implies.

I know darn well that self-taught ethnologist may have fudged a little in his "word-for-word" record of an elder's lecture to young Indians undergoing the coming-of-age ceremony. Gordon knows it, too. I wouldn't be a bit surprised if he did a little revision of his own.

That's what makes this essay, like his others, ring with so much truth.

There are bird-song rattles made out of ancient cottonwood, smoothed by an honored grandfather's knife, worn to fit his hand—and then there are bird-song rattles thrown together in the heat of the moment around a campfire, just an old beer can full of pebbles, a stick, and some duct tape.

The secret that good bird singers all know is that, while an heirloom instrument is nice, it's the song that matters. It's the song that can't, ever, tell a lie.

Nimasianexelpasaleki, Gordon. Your songs make my heart happy. May they go out into the world and find the ears that need to hear them, find homes in hungry hearts, and continue this work of rebuilding the California Indian world.

kolo,
Deborah A. Miranda

Columns and Essays

LOSS OF A FRIEND BRINGS MEMORIES

I'm dialing the way-back machine to circa 1975.

On Sundays Ed Arviso, Ronnie Powvall, and I would be hungover. We lived in a small house on Grape Street in Escondido. In the fridge there would be ice water in a brown ceramic jug with a cork stopper, the kind of jug a hillbilly might drink corn liquor from.

In the fridge, there would be a length of bologna, the kind encased in a red plastic wrapper, bought from Poor Ol' Rube's, a now defunct grocery store.

There would be a block of commodity cheese that Ronnie had gotten from his sister, Debbie.

And there might be some white bread or a pack of tortillas or, if nothing else, soda crackers. We'd slice the bologna and cheese to make breakfast sandwiches, pour a glass of ice water, maybe scarf some cold fries left over from a night-before stop at Jack in the Box, and watch football. For some reason, Ed was a Washington Redskins fan, and he'd whoop at touchdowns and scream at refs for bad calls.

It was a dark time in Ed's life. His wife had left him, and because he still loved her, it kicked him in the heart. He did his best to keep his inner turmoil to himself, but every now and then, his loss would get the better of him, and his eyes would get rusty with tears.

Ed was a big guy, over 6 foot, probably 280 pounds, a standout football player in high school.

He'd been deputized by the San Diego County Sheriff's Department but was conflicted about the job. Faced with the prospect of locking up friends, relatives, and fellow Indians, he walked away from the department.

He was enrolled in the Rincon Reservation but had blood ties to Pechanga, where his father's people were from.

After his wife left, he invited Ronnie to set up camp in the spare bedroom. I was friends with Ronnie, and somehow I ended up surfing the couch. For years afterward, Ed would harp on me for borrowing his socks.

Eventually, Ronnie and I rented the house in front of Ed's house. The three of us hung out together. We were young, we caroused the bars, we did our best to pick up women at nightspots, went to ball games, made road trips to other reservations.

Once we took off in Ronnie's Ford LTD to attend a funeral on the Quechan Reservation near Yuma, Arizona. It was the kind of funeral where they built a pyre and burned the body. But at the same time as the funeral, there was a fiesta going on. We never made it to the funeral.

Once, the National Congress of American Indians convened at the Sheraton Hotel in Escondido, and we all got rooms. The Miss NCAI competition was part of the convention, so pretty contestants populated the lobby and roamed hallways. Ed hosted a lively after-hours party in his room. Suffice it to say no formal charges were levied. And that's all I'm going to say about that.

It wasn't all wildness. We had our business side, too. Ronnie and I worked as proposal writers for the California Tribal Chairmen's

Association. Ed was launching what would become one of the biggest employment training programs for Indians in the county, the Indian Action Team. Eventually, I ended up working for Ed, first as a trainee carpenter, then as a proposal writer.

He was a good boss. When Ed belly-laughed, it was boisterous and joyful, his eyes squinting to the point of practically disappearing. He had the most colorful way of speaking of anyone I ever knew. He came up with the "eyes getting rusted over from tears" saying. He was a master of metaphor.

He put his social skills into play in the business world. Ed Arviso was very good at making his own way in the world.

But nothing lasts forever. Ronnie Powvall died of cancer years ago. Ed Arviso died Wednesday, leaving behind a wife and three daughters.

Once, we were three buddies cruising desert highways, radio blasting, at eighty-five miles per hour in a Ford LTD.

And now no más.

February 11, 2014

LUISEÑO INITIATION

There are times when I've sat at the patio bar of the Bank of Mexican Food, sipped a Negra Modelo, munched on tortilla chips and salsa, and wondered in silence where I went wrong.

I imagine we all feel adrift at times, like we've made a bad turn and are butting heads against a dead end in the labyrinth of life. When I feel the swirl of the world, the chaos of a million bits of information trying to infiltrate my brain, when I feel lost, I revert to simplicity. That's been my lifelong pattern: start out in simplicity, let the complexities pile on until it gets crazy, then return to simplicity.

I know, it's all pretty vague. Maybe I've been reading too much Henry James lately and his style is subverting my own. What I'm trying to say is we all need an anchor, something that tethers us, directs us to do what's right.

I'm a reader, so it makes sense that one of my anchors was found in a book: *The Culture of the Luiseño Indians* by Philip Stedman Sparkman, University of California Publications in American Archaeology and Ethnology, volume 8, 1908.

In the late 1890s, Sparkman, a quiet storekeeper near the Rincon Indian Reservation, learned the Luiseño language, to the point where he compiled a dictionary. He studied Luiseño culture, acquainting himself with many ceremonies. At one initiation ceremony, he wrote down word-for-word a lecture given by elders to young men as they were being initiated into manhood. It should be noted that initiation ceremonies were also conducted for girls transitioning into womanhood.

I was born too late for an initiation ceremony. Although I've heard of a couple attempts at revival, the last "official" initiation ceremony was held in the 1940s.

For both girls and boys, the initiation was a complex, multi-day ordeal that often involved imbibing toloache, a hallucinogenic drink made from a local plant. I won't name the plant because too many youths try it on their own and end up in the hospital.

The ceremony also included a fire dance accompanied by trance-induced visions of animal spirits that might become personal power guides.

Initiates fasted and bathed each morning in cold water, then their bodies were painted. Ground paintings were used to explain the Luiseño cosmology.

Girls were often buried up to their necks in pits for three days, fasting except for sips of water and atole, a thin gruel made from acorns.

Sometimes the boys' ceremony was capped with an ant ordeal: initiates placed in a pit with fire ants that repeatedly bit them. Attendants would stir up the ants to make them mad and bite some more.

There are accounts of boys being whipped with stinging nettles to toughen them for life's hardships.

And there were also reports of a kind of branding with crumpled mugwort placed on the arm and then lit on fire to sear the skin. The burn was left untreated and would subsequently scar.

At the heart of the initiation ceremony was the lecture on how to conduct oneself in the right way. This was the lecture transcribed by Sparkman.

The lecture is too long to recount here, but its prescriptions and admonitions for a good life stay with me to this day.

Here's a much abbreviated sampling of advice given to youngsters on how to live life:

Respect for others is key. Believe in people, and they will see this respect and feel this respect in you, and you will gain fame and be praised.

The earth, the sky, the mountains see you. If you maintain respect for them, you will grow old, and you will pass this respect on to your sons and daughters, and they in turn will pass it along. It's up to the older to teach the younger.

The code teaches generosity. If you kill a rabbit or a deer, willingly share it with others. Don't be angry when you give it. And you will be praised, and you will be able to shoot straight in the future.

Don't steal food, don't eat too fast, don't eat too much, and don't be lazy. Bathe in the early morning and be active during the day and you will win races.

Heed these words and you'll grow old, and people will say you escaped death and went to the sky to become a star.

But ignore these words and you will die and "your spirit (heart) will not rise to the north, nor your soul (towish) to the sky."

When I recall these words, I embrace the teachings of the old ones. I find comfort in these simple virtues. I take another sip of Negra Modelo, and I'm heartened.

April 15, 2014

AN UNKNOWN CONNECTION TO THE PAST

Funny how seemingly insignificant events can snowball.

The other day I got a LinkedIn message from Bryn (rhymes with Lynn) Potter, a woman I didn't know. She had just read my book *Rez Dogs Eat Beans* and wanted to ask me some questions about my great-grandmother Esperanza Fidelio, who I talked about in the book.

My great-grandmother was a basketmaker, and Bryn is working on a book of Southern California Indian basketry and wondered if I could provide further information. I wanted to help if I could, so I called her.

During our conversation, I discovered she's helping to assemble a Cahuilla basket exhibit for the Riverside Metropolitan Museum set to open in September. She's also working to update and expand an older book called *Rods, Bundles & Stitches: A Century of Southern California Indian Basketry*.

This book is apparently the bible of local basketry. And my great-grandmother is in it. As an aside, it's out of print, so if you spot it at a swap meet or thrift store or yard sale, snatch it up. It's easily worth two hundred dollars now, and continues to rise in value.

As we talked, Bryn told me she used to work for the Southwest Museum of the American Indian, specializing in basketry. Curious, she looked up my great-grandmother's name through the museum's website and hit on more than twenty photos of Esperanza, shot between 1927 and 1936.

After our talk, I visited theautry.org. (The Autry Museum has taken over the Southwest Museum. It's complicated.) I clicked over to online collections and entered Esperanza's name into the search engine. The first picture I found was a shot of my great-grandmother next to a woodpile, kneeling over a metate. Standing next to her was my mother, Barbara (Magee) Johnson, at about age four.

It's a picture I'd never seen before.

Esperanza died in the late forties. I wasn't born until 1951, so I never met her. But growing up, I listened to countless stories from my grandmother and my mother about Esperanza, so I feel I almost knew her.

My mother lived in the small shack next door and spent much time with her. She often told of going with her grandmother to the San Luis Rey River, which runs through the Pala Indian Reservation, to collect grasses for basket making. My mother learned to pick grasses, how to soak them, and, while seated next to her grandmother, how to weave the tight coils that would grow into a basket.

My mother often stayed with her grandmother and would complain about being so cold in the thin-walled shack, the wind slipping through cracks, as she tried to sleep beneath threadbare blankets. And she'd sneak into her grandmother's bed and warm her frozen feet against her grandmother's back.

For a time, my great-grandmother and her husband, Pedro Trujillo, raised chilies, and my mother helped to string them and hang them to dry for use in winter stews.

Pedro died young, and Esperanza, husbandless, set up housekeeping with a man named (I think) Epiphano Fidelio. The reservation knew him as Jack Johnson, because he resembled the boxer. We knew him simply as Uncle Jack.

He was my great-grandmother's common-law husband and lived with the family in their small house, even after she died in the late forties. He slept in a small back bedroom, a place of mystery for me, for Uncle Jack was a man of power, and there were things—like crystals under his pillow—that you weren't to touch, or some of the power could bounce back on you and maybe make you sick, or loosen your teeth, or cause you to fall off a roof.

It was said he used his power mostly for good, for healing, but you never knew.

To us kids, Uncle Jack seemed a gruff man. My Uncle Copy tells the story of getting whipped by Uncle Jack with his belt for fighting with a younger cousin.

"He was strict," my uncle said. Now he can laugh about it. I don't think he thought it was funny back then.

After my great-grandmother died, my Aunt Clara and Uncle Jack used to drink wine in the shade of an old tree at the side of the house, and they could be heard laughing the afternoon away. When I was about ten years old, my cousin Randy discovered Uncle Jack dead in the outhouse, his heart refusing to take one more beat. Uncle Jack was one of those people in my life that I always wished I knew better.

My great-grandmother died a long, slow, painful death of stomach cancer. My mother often rubbed her stomach for her. "Oh, girlie, your hands feel so good," she'd say.

My Uncle Copy sat at my computer, and we looked at the old photos. He'd comment: "There's the house where I was born," "That's me in that cradleboard," and "I'm sure that's my mother."

And the memories flooded in. All because of a LinkedIn message from Bryn Potter. Thanks, Bryn.

April 25, 2014

REFLECTING ON A LIFE

In his bedroom on the Pala Indian Reservation, his old marriage bed has been replaced by a hospital bed, where he now spends his hours in striped sheets, propped up on pillows, staring at a white ceiling fan.

There's a new flat-screen TV mounted to the wall, but it's turned off. He finds his memories provide better company.

On a table near his bed, there's an abalone shell with a bundle of dried sage wrapped in red yarn. The tip of the sage has been burned to smudge the room. A set of antlers from a young buck sits nearby.

Richard "Onnie" Mojado (he spells it Onnie, but it's pronounced Oonie) has pancreatic cancer. He's in hospice care. Maybe the word *hospice* has a softer sound than *hospital*, but the meaning is less than comforting. It portends the end.

His bedroom window is open. Sounds of the outer world seep in: the whir of cars on Highway 76, the occasional yip from a passel of rez puppies tugging on one another's ears, a crow scolding from a nearby tree.

In the next room, his daughter, Trina, watches TV and talks on the phone. Every now and then she checks on his comfort, brings him a plastic cup of grape juice with a flexible straw.

Onnie is seventy-two but looks older. Once a 280-pound man, strong, handsome in a black cowboy hat with a beaded hatband, he's now a desiccated version of his former self. Cancer knows no mercy.

I've known Onnie for most of my life. Way back when I played fast-pitch softball for the Pala men's team, Onnie was my coach. We've played on the same peon team off and on for more than thirty years. He's godfather to my youngest son, Bear.

He's a family man. His wife, Brenda, died several years ago, but he has Trina, and a son, Lawrence, and five grandchildren.

He worked twenty-seven years for the Fallbrook sanitation department, and after retiring from there he worked four years for tribal maintenance, and another five as security for Pala Casino.

He's gonna die on the reservation where he was born. He wouldn't have it otherwise. In quiet moments, the ceiling fan spins images from his life.

He sees the cup he drank coffee in as a kid. He drank it sweet but with no milk. Lactose intolerance is common with Indians.

"Coffee for breakfast, coffee for dinner. It's mostly what we drank," he says. "And we had a lot of mush for breakfast. No steak and eggs in those days."

Sometimes the fan spins him a rabbit sitting in a clearing in between sage and chamise, his iron-sighted .22-caliber rifle trained on what was just a trigger squeeze away from becoming dinner. He'd carry them home by their hind legs so his mom, Dorothy, could fry them up in a cast-iron frying pan.

"Dang they were good," he says.

Once his Uncle Porky bought him a fielder's glove, a Spalding. You couldn't give a kid who loved sports as much as Onnie anything better. He rubbed it down with neatsfoot oil until it was soft as an earlobe. He shoveled in many a ground ball at shortstop with that glove, snagged many a line drive in the outfield with it.

After high school, he joined the army, stationed at Fort Ord and Hunter Liggett. He's proud of his military service and active in local veterans' affairs.

Onnie grew up across the street from Brenda, the girl he would marry. They were high school sweethearts. She went to college in Utah, eventually got her master's degree, and headed up the Pala Head Start program for thirty-eight years. All four of my kids went to Head Start; all four learned to read from "Teacher Brenda."

Sometimes, this fan spins visions of his brother and sister, now dead, playing in the yard, or his children opening Christmas presents, or his wife singing Indian songs; she had a lovely voice.

He took his last drink about forty years ago. He simply quit when he found that drink was interfering with family.

Onnie liked to travel with his family. He usually bought a big van, large enough for them to be comfortable in. They made summer trips to Fort Duchesne powwows in Utah, where Brenda was originally from.

"I loved going to those," he says.

They traveled as a family to peon games all around Southern California and Arizona reservations. They liked to eat at Denny's while on the road.

When we played peon, an Indian bone game, Onnie usually anchored one end, while I had the other. King Freeman and John Chutnicutt would take the inside positions. Later his son played too, father and son singing in unison.

Onnie has a distinctive singing voice, clear and resonant. Of all our team members, Onnie was the one most likely to go on a run. He was Coyote, fooling opponents into thinking he was hiding one way, but smiling when showing them they were wrong. There was seldom a game when he didn't have at least one good run.

Onnie has had a good run. He tries to be philosophical about the unavoidable end. Maybe he'll just fall asleep and not wake up. It can happen any time, he says.

"I don't think about death much. I think about life, all that I've done, all the people I've known, all the good and bad times I've had."

And he has his faith. Most Sunday mornings he could be found at the Pala Mission's Mass. Father Rey still brings him communion.

I ask him, "So what was most important?"

Without hesitation, he says, "My family. Keeping my family strong, everyone going in the right direction."

You hear a lot of talk these days about what a real man is. To me, that's a real man.

May 23, 2014

MEMORIES OF MISSION SAN ANTONIO DE PALA

Rain Bird sprinklers twitch over the front landscape of Mission San Antonio de Pala. June sunbeams play in the spray like a Horace Silver jazz riff. The morning air is cool, damp; the red and purple geraniums drink it all in.

A white campanile with its double-decker bells stands above it all. But it's a tower of confusion, a symbol of mixed feelings. Below the bell tower, a red-winged blackbird lands on the circular river-rock wall that serves as a planting bed for flowers. These days roses, daisies, and poppies splash color on what I remember was once the mission fountain.

When I was a kid, koi and goldfish called the fountain home. I used to like to watch flashes of gold and calico fin through the algae-green water. The fountain also served as a wishing well. Tourists and locals alike would close their eyes tight, make wishes, and toss coins into the fountain. Silver coins would flicker through the green water on their way to the bottom.

I guess the idea was that this was blessed ground, and wishes made here had a better chance of being granted. I don't know if the wishes ever came true. But I think it's a matter of mathematics that at least a few did.

When the fountain got too choked with green, the mission priest would put out a call to rez boys to clean it out. The summer sun would sting our shoulders as we sat to remove our Converse high-tops. We'd jump into the water in our cutoffs to pluck coins from the muck and try to remove the algae, which slipped through our fingers like overcooked spinach.

The priest would stand by in black pants and a white T-shirt with a bucket for us to drop the coins in. It was odd to see him so casual. For us boys it was a romp.

Nobody on the reservation had a pool back then. If you were lucky, you'd sit in a galvanized washtub in the front yard or in a horse trough in the barn lot to cool off. Climbing into the fountain was the closest most of us kids got to splashing in a pool.

The priest kept most of the coins, but after we'd cleaned the fountain as good as we could, he'd give us a few. It was crazy-good to feel them jangling in your wet pocket. We'd race across the street to the Pala Store and buy treats. One of my favorites was a bag of peanuts dumped into a bottle of Pepsi. I liked to see the salt fizz. I liked the taste of Pepsi-soaked peanuts as well.

The Pala Mission was built in 1816 with Indian labor under Padre Antonio Peyri, a Franciscan priest. Peyri is credited with founding the mission, actually an asistencia to Mission San Luis Rey in Oceanside, but it was Indians who mixed the mud and straw to form the adobes.

They cut timbers with handsaws on Palomar Mountain and dragged them with horses to form the rafters. In many places, the walls of stacked adobe bricks are more than four feet thick. It was hard work, sometimes done under the sting of a lash.

My grandparents were married in the mission. So were my parents. So was I. My kids have all been baptized in the mission. My grandmother went to Mass there every morning. But I seldom go to Mass there anymore. The mission, however, endures.

June 20, 2014

A PART OF RESERVATION LIFE

When I was seven or eight, back when cattle grazed much of the local countryside and pickups outnumbered sedans, when most yards had a few chickens pecking for insects, I remember riding with my uncle down Pechanga Road. We were probably taking my grandfather to a Pechanga tribal meeting.

I remember going past the Salgado home and seeing one of the boys, maybe it was GiGi or Gino, carrying a rabbit by the hind legs into the house. He paused for a moment at the door to let little brothers and sisters playing in the yard see what he'd brought home. The image of him standing there, holes in the knees of his jeans, rabbit in hand—the proud hunter—remains fixed in my brain as an iconic reservation image. To me this is what rez life was about in those days.

I wanted so badly to be the proud hunter. I was too young at the time, but the desire to bring home game burned in my innards.

A few years later, I was allowed to roam the Pala Reservation backcountry with my cousins on hunting outings. On the way back we'd be hot and tired. We'd put creek pebbles in our mouths to stave off thirst. Once, we tried cutting open a cactus to get moisture from the paddle, but a snake, a red racer, slithered out and we didn't want any part of that.

I didn't have a gun yet, but they'd let me shoot one of theirs. They'd set up beer cans on a fence, and I'd aim at the center of the red X on Lucky Lager cans.

I was just learning and wasn't much of a shot. But for Christmas when I was eight or nine, I got a lever-action Daisy BB gun. It was the cool kind that resembled a Model 1894 Winchester, the kind cowboys carried in scabbards on horseback. I spent my days honing my shooting skills with that gun. It was *my* gun.

There were big boulders down by the bridge, where lizards liked to hang out. I'd stalk them, stepping slowly and quietly in my Keds, the river-bottom sand muffling any sound. I'd spot one doing push-ups on a rock, raise the BB gun to my shoulder, and place the lizard in the buckhorn sights.

My father was on his college rifle team and was a heck of a shot. He taught me gun safety at a young age. I have an older cousin, Robert Banks, who was a terrific shot. I once saw him hit a jackrabbit on the run. To this day I've never shot a rabbit on the run, but he could do it. He was my idol. I wanted to shoot like him.

When I was old enough, about ten, I started carrying a .22 on hunting outings with my cousins.

Roaming the sage, chaparral, and cactus with a gun in hand, looking for the camouflaged shape of a rabbit hiding in the brush, remains a favorite memory. I'd bring home rabbits—carrying them by the hind legs—and my grandmother would heat her cast-iron frying pan, dip rabbit parts in flour, and fry them in bacon grease.

Back then, money was tight. The extra protein was welcomed. Most Indian boys did the same for their families.

Back then, I never heard of a kid taking a gun to school.

Somewhere along the line, something in society went very wrong. I wish it were otherwise.

It's been a long time since I've been hunting. But there was a time when it was simply a part of life. Once, I loved guns. Today, my feelings are mixed.

September 5, 2014

BEING IN THE SWEAT FOCUSES THE SENSES

Balanced on pitchfork tines, a river rock glowed red with fire-borne heat. Oh so carefully, Frankie Orosco, the fire tender, lowered the football-sized rock through the doorway, setting it in front of Randall "Doc" Majel, the sweat leader. Doc grabbed the rock with forked deer antlers to place it in the center pit.

The lodge, about twelve feet in diameter, was more than ample for the ten of us who were sitting on a ledge carved into earth facing the pit. Above our heads, surplus military canvas stretched over bent willow branches formed a cathedral-like dome.

The flap covering the doorway was folded up, allowing night-cold and firelight to seep in. Once the rocks were in place, though, Frankie lowered the flap, and darkness became tangible, our interiors fusing with lodge interiors. And thusly the sweat began.

We were gathered at my buddy King's house for a New Year's sweat, a thing we've been doing for more than thirty years. But this time we missed New Year's because rain and snow dampened our best intentions, so we settled for a couple of nights after. If the sweat lodge has taught us anything, it's taught us to be flexible.

Doc sprinkled a mix of wild tobacco and sweet grass onto

the hot rocks, and soon the interior filled with sacred smoke, like incense in a confessional. The rocks, which had been scorched in the fire for several hours, hummed with heat and power. The rocks glowed, and through the smoke I could make out the faces of my sweat brothers and sisters, and faces in the rocks themselves, faces of the primordial past.

With a ladle fashioned from a gourd, Doc scooped water from a bucket and splashed it onto the rocks. The water beaded, jumped, sizzled, and steam billowed like a symphony.

I'm gonna stop the description here. I won't recount the prayers of the sweat. What is voiced in the sweat stays in the sweat. It's a shared moment, but a private moment, with a code of silence invoked.

But it's okay if I speak a little of what happens for me inside the sweat. I once heard of life described as "the dance of person and presence."

I examine that phrase in the sweat because there is no place where I am more present. All senses focused on the here and now. I hear the sound of voices raised in ancient songs, the rhythmic explosions of seeds inside gourd rattles, the smells of blistering rocks meeting fresh sage. I feel lightened, purified, made whole. There is a sense of ancestors infusing my being with their wisdom, their strength. And that's just a little of what happens for me.

A couple of months ago, as I walked to my writing shack out back of my house, I happened upon a dead red-shouldered hawk with wings outstretched in the dirt. The hawk must have died in the night, because it wasn't there the day before.

I regarded the hawk as a gift from the Creator, and glanced skyward to say thanks. I cleaved the talons off and dropped them into a Mason jar of alcohol and glycerin, letting them cure for several weeks to preserve them.

Ever since I was a kid, I've felt a kinship with hawks. Every time I've spotted one soaring, heard one keen, watched one dive with talons outstretched, I've felt blessed. Hawks and I have a special relationship.

I wrapped the preserved talons with a length of leather bootlace and gave them to my sons, Brandon and Bear, for Christmas.

It's not easy being a man in this world. I gave them the talons so they might borrow on the hawk's strength and wisdom as they make their way from cradle to grave in a world that doesn't know the meaning of fair or unfair. In the sweat, I prayed for them, for all my loved ones, for all humanity.

I think about things like that in the sweat.

Here's wishing you all strength and good fortune in the coming year.

January 5, 2015

SCHOOL WITH A CONNECTION TO THE PAST

Morning breezes riffle through the American and Californian flags held upright by schoolchildren at Temecula's Helen Hunt Jackson Elementary School.

Students assemble on the asphalt playground, sitting or kneeling on mats dragged out of classrooms for the purpose. Principal Brian Martes, casual in a zip-up sweatshirt, T-shirt, and running shoes, is at the microphone leading the kids in a coyote howl. The coyote is the school mascot.

In the background, chaparral hills punctuated by granite boulders, a landscape where real coyotes roam, occupy the horizon.

Three of my grandchildren attend Jackson elementary. No, I'm not one of those grandfathers who goes on and on about my grandkids' exploits. Suffice it to say, I was there for the Coyote of the Month assembly and, yes, some awards were involved.

But more than that, I was struck by how different the approach to education is today compared with the fifties, when I went to school.

I went to parochial school, where classrooms were ruled by nuns in starched habits.

The nuns in my day were no-nonsense. I don't ever remember an honoring ceremony like this one. And here's what made it different: This assembly wasn't to recognize the best speller, or who could add columns of numbers fastest, or who knew every state in the union.

This assembly was to honor acts of kindness.

Yes, kindness. I doubt kindness was on the radar in my school life in the fifties.

At this assembly, I saw teachers pleasantly conversing with students. After the assembly, I saw Principal Martes sit on the multipurpose-room steps and joke with each honoree, as the beaming student sat next to him.

The gentle approach may not work for every student, but for most, especially my grandchildren, it's nurturing, and I applaud the school for it.

Here's another thing about Helen Hunt Jackson Elementary School: It's named after the woman who wrote the famous book *Ramona*.

And here's something my grandkids don't know: They are related to the woman Helen Hunt Jackson based her Ramona character on—Ramona Lubo.

Ramona Lubo was a Cahuilla woman who watched with her baby in her arms as Sam Temple shot her husband, Juan Diego, in the doorway of their house for stealing a horse. Some say he was shot twenty-two times, but it's difficult to sort through truth and fabrication with the Ramona story.

Ramona was Paul Magee's great-aunt. Paul Magee was my grandfather.

This was a relationship my mother was so proud of. She would regale gas station attendants, as they filled our tank, with tales of Ramona and how she was related.

She loved all things Ramona.

In 1928, the year my mother was born, Dolores del Río starred in a film about Ramona. It had an accompanying song called "Ramona" that became a million seller. My father learned the song and sang it for my mother on special occasions. She cried every time.

Once, we drove to Old Town San Diego so my mother could see the adobe where Ramona and Alessandro were said to have wed.

One birthday I bought my mother a leather-bound edition at a rare-book store.

There's no time to go deeply into the Ramona story here, but someday I'll write more about it.

It seems a quirk of fate that my grandkids go to a school connected to their blood. One day I'll sit them down and try to explain it to them.

Who knows, they might get a kick out of it.

March 4, 2015

ROUNDUP AS IN DAYS OF OLD

Buick-sized boulders, high chaparral, and ancient oaks stud the hills and ravines of the Cahuilla Indian Reservation near Anza.

In a drought-thinned pasture about four hundred yards south of the Clarke family place, a half-dozen or so riders work their way behind the small herd of about sixty. They attempt to slowly move the cattle, in a tight group, toward the corral, where they'll get vaccinated and where spring calves will get branded.

But it's not so easy. Jittery and rebellious, animals break through gaps between riders, juking like halfbacks to head downfield. Cattle-wise quarter horses wheel in chase, hooves digging in, strides lengthening to turn the fleeing beef.

You can hear the yips and hollers of riders brandishing ropes, waving hats, hoping to enforce order. You can hear the cattle snorting and bellowing, unwilling to go meekly.

From folding chairs up near the house, Patsy Liera, seventy-five, and Virginia "Ginger" Liera, eighty, watch the cowboys with a smile. The sights and sounds are all too familiar. As little girls they watched their father and uncles and other local cowboys do the same. And once old enough, they too were atop horses chasing cattle.

"It was a fun way of life," Virginia says.

For nearly a hundred years, the Clarke home has been the site of an annual roundup and branding. At one time there were probably a half-dozen Cahuilla families who raised cattle and had big roundups. While several families still raise cattle, the Clarke-Liera roundup is the last to operate on this scale.

"My dad did it. My grandfather did it. I'm not going to let it die with me," Gerald Clarke says.

Gerald's first cousin, Robert Liera, agrees. Family members share ownership of the herd, and the whole family contributes to the roundup. The night before, a pit is dug and bundles of beef and a couple of turkeys are thrown onto coals, covered, and left to cook overnight.

The kids and other family members all pitch in. Beans and stews and salads are made. Patsy herself made sixty tortillas Friday night.

Even weewish, a traditional but labor-intensive Indian staple made from acorn flour, is prepared. Gerald's daughters helped shell and grind the acorns.

It takes some doing, but most of the cattle are eventually driven into the corral and the gate is closed.

A couple of runaways go "na-na-na" out in the pasture. "Yeah, they're laughing now, but they'll be first to go to market," Clarke says. "Cows like that rile up the others."

Cowboys, and one cowgirl, use their horses to separate out the adults, aiming them through a chute where Gerald jabs them with a big hypodermic full of medicines to keep them healthy.

When Clarke isn't cowboying, he's an artist and is head of the visual arts department at Idyllwild Arts Academy. When Robert Liera isn't cowboying, he works helping to keep the Pauma casino running smoothly.

One by one, each calf is roped, then stretched out to get

earmarked, inoculated, and branded. Branding irons are heated in a fire. And all twenty-five calves get their mark.

Family and friends help with the work. It takes some doing to drop a squalling calf on its side and hold it there while it gets doctored and branded.

But once the work is done, the feasting starts. The feed is part of the tradition, Patsy says. They put on a big spread back when she was little, too. Her uncle, John Lubo, would grow grapes and make wine. The wine flowed with dinner.

It's always worrisome how the meat will turn out. But when the burlap is removed from the bundle, and the aluminum foil is slit open, sweet steam rises from the beef stewing in its own juices. And you know it's gonna be good.

Prayers are offered, and a hundred or so people sit down to eat a meal that could have been served a hundred years ago.

June 8, 2015

WAITING ALL YEAR FOR THE RINCON FIESTA

Long and low, the Rincon Reservation Tribal Hall in northern San Diego County occupied a weedy lot just off the paved highway.

For most of the year, it was a bare-bones meeting hall, the place where people argued about water rights and complained about unfenced cattle roaming loose in backyard gardens.

It was old, arthritic, the roofline sagging like a swayback horse. But come fiesta time, the old hall perked up, stood taller, energized, ready to dance.

To prepare the grounds, men cut willows with machetes in the San Luis Rey River bottom for ramadas. They'd frame the ramadas with poles, and string up wire so lengths of willow could be woven in.

Some ramadas were used as poker dens, where people bet on busted flushes while draining whiskeys—a buck a shot. Most, however, served as restaurants.

Families equipped them with gas stoves where tamales were steamed and hamburger meat was fried, and frybread bubbled in oil. Tables and chairs were set up out front so diners could sit while eating tacos so lush the hamburger grease dribbled down wrists.

You haven't lived until you've dived into a breakfast of chorizo and eggs, or a steaming bowl of menudo topped with diced onions and oregano, after a long fiesta night.

People waited all year for it. A fiesta fever grabbed hold. Teens couldn't sit still at the dinner table. Women would appraise new dance moves in the mirror. Men thumbed through greenbacks socked away in top drawers. A man needed some cash in his pocket to bet on a peon game or to buy his best girl a beer and combo tortilla roll.

The night before fiesta, young bucks in old trucks with Redbone's "Come and Get Your Love" blasting on the eight-track would lean out of windows screaming, "Fiesta, fiesta, fiesta!" Young girls would start mentally assembling the right outfit, something to catch the eye, but something that wouldn't show the dirt.

If nothing else, fiesta was dusty. And at fiesta, anything could happen. You just didn't know.

The heart of fiesta was the dance. The hall had a wood floor worn smooth by countless boots doing the Rincon Stomp. The band played the front of the room. In the bar in back, Ed Arviso and Berkeley Calac would sell you beers—buck a beer. The ceiling was open and rock 'n' roll bounced in the rafters.

There was a mandatory playlist. Every fiesta band had to know "Brown Eyed Girl," "Knock on Wood," and some Freddy Fender tunes like "I Love My Rancho Grande." Lines of dancers would hook arms, corrido-style, and dance toward each other, and then veer off just before colliding. And people would laugh and holler after a near miss.

Fiesta was geared for all ages. They might play an old swing song so older folks could boogie-woogie. And many could do the Stroll. Two lines would form and couples would stroll down the middle.

Some of those couples had been strolling for many years. They'd look into each other's eyes while dancing, and there was something long-lasting and romantic about it.

Today, the old hall is gone. The new grounds don't have the same magic for me. Plus, I'm getting a little long in the tooth for fiesta.

July 13, 2015

SOMETHING TO BELIEVE IN

Most Southern California Indians have no trouble believing in spirits. Many ceremonies and rituals exist to appease the dead—to keep them from mingling with the living.

In the old days, before houses got too expensive, homes would be purposely burned to the ground when someone died. With no home, with no belongings to come back for, the dead would be less likely to visit.

Burning of the Clothes, a ceremony held to this day, occurs for basically the same reason. Friends and family gather and sing mourning songs as items of clothing are brought out from closets and thrown onto a pyre. The leather coat worn to football games, the Levi's jacket worn on deer hunts, favorite cowboy boots worn at fiesta dances. Same goes for women: Sunday dresses, comfy Uggs, the jewelry box her daddy gave her when she was a girl.

All go up in flames.

Before the arrival of missionaries, Southern California Indians often burned their dead. With no earthly body, there was even less reason for the dead to visit earth.

At the velorios (wakes), fabric—often black—is tacked over windows in the room where the casket awaits. The fabric keeps unwanted spirits out while the soul of the departed ascends to its final place in the firmament. In the old Indian way, souls become stars in the night sky, forever burning, forever watchful.

So you see, practically from infancy, the notion of spirits is culturally accepted.

I say these things as background, as a way to put the following story into context.

About seventy years ago, in the high backcountry of the Santa Ysabel Indian Reservation in San Diego County, Julio and Lena Guachino lived with their many kids in a remote log cabin away from everyone.

Santa Ysabel is a mountain reservation where the houses are isolated. Trees are a mix of oaks, conifers, and sycamores, and thick brush mixed with open grassy meadows covers the hillsides. Santa Ysabel is good deer country, good cattle country.

It was snowing that day, but Julio and Lena needed to drive to Ramona for staples. They loaded the kids into the car, except Ralph, who was maybe eleven, and Joe, who was maybe thirteen, both old enough to be home alone.

With snow falling, the brothers huddled around the wood stove, feeding it oak logs, trying to stay warm. The fire popped and snapped, but then they heard something else: someone walking outside. Sure, the footsteps in the snow were muffled, but the icy crunch was clearly audible.

Joe, the older brother, always quick to act, went for his dad's deer rifle. Later in life he was known as the guy who'd rip off his shirt at the first sign of a fistfight. Even in his sixties, he was once umping a softball game on the La Jolla Reservation when a young gun got into his face over a disputed call. Rather than engage in a prolonged argument, Joe balled up his fist and dropped the upstart with one punch. Joe was that kind of guy.

Anyway, they heard footsteps. Joe had the gun; Ralph picked up a shovel.

"Who is it? Who's there?" they called out.

No one answered.

Ralph took the lantern to the window to see if he could see anyone.

But no sign of anyone.

Then a loud thump, like someone had fallen against the house. The cabin door shook, as if someone was trying to get in.

"I've got a gun!" Joe yelled. "I'll shoot!"

Ralph, still peering out the window, thought he saw a car coming up the drive. Mom and Dad, he thought. They opened the door to welcome the safety of their parents, but there was no car, no person, no nothing, only trackless snow.

Time passed in fear. The stove, even with a full load of wood, couldn't keep the trembles at bay. More noise at the door. Joe held up the big lever-action gun, ready to shoot.

The door opened. Their dad, Julio, hollered out, "Hey, it's us!"

A mix of relief and horror. Mom and Dad were home, but they almost got shot.

After a while, Ralph rechecked the window. He spotted a coin on the outside windowsill and a handprint on the glass, as if whoever set the coin there had leaned against the glass.

Ralph and Joe were shaking and scared witless as they told of the intruder. Julio walked with them around the house, but there were no footprints, no signs of anyone.

To this day it remains a mystery.

Ralph and Joe have been dead many years. But I knew them well. They were men of tradition, respected peon players and bird singers. Ralph told this story to his daughter Lela Guachino of Pala when she was about fifteen. She's in her fifties now. Lela told this story to me the other day.

"I loved listening to his stories," Lela said. "This one was a little spooky and made me curious about the spirit world."

"And heck yes, I believe in spirits," she said.

October 26, 2015

A REZ TAKE ON MISSION FOODS

Much of life is a search for home, a desire to belong.

For me, there is no better expression of home than the foods of my childhood: tacos, burritos, enchiladas, tamales, empanadas, palillis, and the rest—all foods that got passed from the missions through the Indian generations to me.

So, as others debate the damages missions have wrought on California Indian culture, allow me to sink my teeth into a greasy taco, juices from tomatoes, salsa, fried hamburger oozing from the bottom, running down my arm, dripping onto my shirt.

It's partly why you see so many Indians with stains on their ribbon shirts at gatherings.

Would there be tacos here without the missions? Sure. But for those of us who grew up in the shade of mission campaniles, tacos and other mission foods have become our destiny.

On the Pala Indian Reservation where I live, home to Mission San Antonio de Pala, an asistencia of Mission San Luis Rey, many locals don't attend the mission's Sunday Mass. Nearly all, however, crave the modern-day offspring of mission foods.

Mission foods nourish our bellies as well as our souls.

True, mission padres and Spanish soldiers often dealt cruelly, sometimes unmercifully, with California Indians. But there is no denying that missions and ranchos left a lasting imprint on our culinary selves.

Before the missions, we Indians led confined culinary lives. Coastal natives hunted and gathered. They shot deer, speared fish, collected wild greens, ground acorns into flour.

Before the missions, acorns were a staple. Up and down the coast, where great oaks flourished, Indians picked acorns to make a kind of gruel.

Each tribe had a different name for it. On the Pala Indian Reservation, the Cupeño, Luiseño, and Diegueño Indians who live here call the acorn pudding weewish.

In the fall, when acorns dropped from the trees, the people bent to pluck them from the ground. The deer liked acorns too, so it was an annual contest to see who got the most.

Pre-mission Indians stored the acorns in big twig-woven granaries. I'm sure it was some kid's job to run to the kuulish (the granary) and fetch a basketful of acorns for his mother so she could grind the meats into flour.

The flour had to be thoroughly washed to leach it of residual tannins, the same tannins the padres found useful for tanning hides. After leaching, the flour was boiled into a pudding-like dish, resembling a thick Hawaiian poi.

While weewish is nutritious, packed with proteins, vitamins, and other nutrients, it's not what you'd call bursting with flavor.

Don't get me wrong. I like weewish. But I like it best when it's sopping up bean juice, nicely salted, and topped with good, hot salsa.

On its own, it's bland. Some newbies liken it to mud. Few kids these days like it. And I'm guessing, in the olden days, after eating it day after day, no kid, when Mom told him there was weewish for dinner, jumped with glee singing, "Weewish, weewish, we all wish for weewish."

Man doesn't live by weewish alone.

Enter Mission San Diego de Alcalá, the first mission, founded by Father Junípero Serra in 1769.

In addition to Catholic guilt, the mission introduced local Indians to a sacred vegetable—the chili pepper. Indian life was forever changed.

The missionaries brought with them some twenty-five chili varieties, including piquín, ancho, serrano, guero, poblano, and chipotle, each offering a slightly different taste explosion.

I wasn't there at the time, but I gotta think an Indian subsisting on plain venison, boiled or roasted, all his life must have experienced a transcendental awakening at the first taste of beef slowly simmered in a thick, spicy red chili sauce—a moment of pure incendiary pleasure.

Red Chili Sauce

¼ cup fat (shortening or lard)
2 cups red chili pulp
1 medium onion
1 clove of garlic
¼ teaspoon oregano
½ teaspoon salt
1 tablespoon flour
¼ cup water

Before I was born, my grandmother Delfreda Trujillo Magee went every Saturday with her mother, Esperanza Trujillo, to clean the mission in preparation for Sunday Mass. On Sunday they would go to Mass. Later in life, my grandmother went to Mass every day, and wore out her prayer books and rosary beads at home. My grandmother was thoroughly missionized.

Before I was born, she cooked on a woodburning stove in a two-room shack. But shortly after World War II, she and my grandfather, Paul Magee, a Cahuilla from the Pechanga Indian Reservation, commenced building a small adobe house, making the bricks from scratch, friends and relatives supplying labor.

The house sported a butane stove, my grandmother's first modern appliance. There was always a box of wooden kitchen matches handy to light the burners. Early-morning kitchen sounds included my grandmother scratching the match head on the matchbox striker. Then a slow twist of the handle, the soft whoosh of the ignited burner, the clank of cast iron on the burner grill.

My grandmother cooked primarily with cast iron.

In photos of restored mission kitchens, the white-plastered walls are festooned with cast-iron pots and pans used some two hundred years ago. Makes sense that Indians would get the cast-iron habit. And why not? Cast iron retains heat well and, if properly cured, is as nonstick as Teflon, and, unlike Teflon, it lasts forever. I have a couple of my grandmother's frying pans and they're still usable after more than eighty years of frying eggs and bacon.

In fact, most Pala women of my grandmother's generation cooked with cast iron on cast-iron cookstoves.

In the fifties, however, many women, like my mother, Barbara (Magee) Johnson, strayed from cast iron for a time. As a wedding gift, she received a set of copper-bottomed Revere Ware pots and pans. And she cooked with them, thinking that's what the modern fifties housewife was supposed to do. But the eggs stuck to the bottom, they required Brillo Pads and elbow grease to clean, and they didn't distribute heat evenly.

Eventually, she reverted to cast iron, like her mamma taught her.

Tacos

1½ pounds ground beef
2 fresh tomatoes
1 medium onion
1 clove of garlic
⅛ teaspoon thyme
salt and pepper

My grandmother had a small cast-iron frying pan she used for deep-frying corn tortillas. In another cast-iron frying pan she fried the hamburger, garlic, onions, and other taco ingredients.

My grandmother had never heard of Taco Tuesday; just about any night was a good taco night. She heated oil, usually just Wesson oil or Rex lard, until it almost, but not quite, smoked. With the oil hot, she'd slip in a corn tortilla and let it bubble. It didn't take long. She preferred her tacos softer, not too crispy. But enough resistance in the bite to offer a little crunch.

She liked to drink a little beer when she cooked, and there was often a tall can of Lucky Lager next to the stove for sipping on between the stories she'd tell if you happened to be in the kitchen with her.

When I was a much younger guy, I hung out in her kitchen as she cooked, my fingers perched above the keys of a small typewriter on her Formica kitchen table. As I worked on short stories, I got to smell the garlic mingling with the onions in the frying hamburger. The smell of hamburger frying in onion and garlic not only makes me salivate, it's a time machine transporting me back to my grandmother's kitchen.

To spice up her tacos, she liked to make a hot chili salsa in a molcajete, a small stone grinding bowl used with a pestle. Somewhere along the line, she lost her pestle and used a river rock about the right size instead. She ground dried red peppers into flakes, adding cloves of garlic and tomato sauce. She left in the seeds because they provided heat. The chilies plus the tomato sauce would turn a rich, almost mahogany red.

She'd cut some lettuce, dice some tomatoes, and grate some cheese, usually from a block of commodity cheese, the government cheese that has achieved almost cult status on Indian reservations. It got so I liked commodity cheese on my tacos.

Back in the mission days, neophytes—the Indians who worked at the missions and learned the religion—would do all the cooking. Back then, corn tortillas were made from nixtamal. This was produced from dried corn in a process learned from Indians at missions in Mexico. They'd take a gallon of water, two quarts of dry corn, a quarter cup of unslaked lime, and let it simmer for half an hour until the hulls of the corn could be removed. Then they would wash the corn to remove all traces of lime, and grind it into masa, a kind of a corn dough. The masa was then flattened into tortillas.

My grandmother was more modern. She'd just send me to the Pala Store to buy corn tortillas.

She didn't really make her own chili sauce either, although she could have. Instead, she usually just used canned Las Palmas or El Pato sauce and added Gebhardt chili powder to bump up the heat.

She didn't make her own tamale masa either. I'd drive her to a little Mexican market in Escondido where she'd buy fresh masa from their refrigerated section. Before I could drive, someone else would drive her. My grandmother never got behind the wheel of anything that I know of.

The Pala Reservation has known many expert tamale makers, my grandmother among them. I preferred my grandmother's tamales above all others, but then I had a bias.

Tamales weren't just a Christmas treat; she made them on occasion throughout the year. But tamales were labor intensive, so they were more often reserved for special days.

Tamales were a big part of Christmas cheer. She'd trim a chuck roast or pork butt of fat, brown it, then braise it with onions, garlic, maybe a little oregano, salt, and pepper, until the meat was super tender, usually a couple of hours.

Then she'd simmer the meat in a chili sauce, usually Las Palmas or El Pato diluted with water. Many people add cumin at this point, but my grandmother never did. Probably why, to this day, I don't care much for cumin.

She'd set up an assembly line, spooning masa into soaked corn husks, adding the meat filling, and lastly an olive, kind of like the prize in a Cracker Jack box, then roll them into tight cylinders, tying the ends with little strands of corn husk. My grandmother's tamales were always rolled, never folded.

She had a big blue enamel tamale pot with a lid. In it, she'd steam the tamales, adding a little Las Palmas to the water.

On Christmas Eve, the house windows would cloud with condensation from the tamale pot on the stove. After Midnight Mass, we'd come home to a warm house, my grandfather's oak fire glowing in the fireplace, the kitchen warmed by tamale smells, an aromatic blending of chili meat, masa, and corn husks.

Carolers in thick jackets and ankle-length coats would sing out front and my grandmother would invite them in for tamales and hot coffee brewed in a big metal pot, the kind where the coffee percolated into a glass bulb in the lid.

Friends and family and carolers would talk, laugh, and hum over bowls of tamales while wishing each other Merry Christmas.

Palillis

> 3 cups unbleached all-purpose flour
> 3 teaspoons baking powder
> 1 teaspoon salt
> 3 tablespoons fat (shortening or lard)
> 1 to 1¼ cups PET evaporated milk
> 1 quart cooking oil

At contemporary powwows, people line up for Indian tacos made from frybread. Palillis are a mission/rancho style of frybread. There are variations on the frybread theme all over Indian Country, we just happen to call them palillis.

Hot out of the frying pan, topped with a little powdered sugar or honey, they make a three-star dessert. For a savory approach, add meat and beans and cheese, lettuce, tomato, and salsa—voilà, an Indian taco.

I loved my grandmother's palillis, golden and light. When you bit into them, hot grease seemed to squirt from the fried dough. They were good with sugar or honey. Today, you might even spread Nutella on them, but I liked them best with beans refried in bacon grease, a little cheese, and some hot sarsa.

In mission country, salsa is better known as sarsa. I don't know why, but that's how it's pronounced. It just kind of evolved that way. And everyone has their own take on how to make it: from mild to melt-your-face hot; fresh tomatoes or canned; some use cilantro, some use cumin, some use garlic.

My grandfather was the sarsa maker in our house. He considered cumin and garlic in sarsa sacrilegious. On hot summer days, he liked to be in the shade of the big ash tree out front, seated at an old kitchen table and chair, listening to a ball game on his transistor radio, dicing jalapeño and yellow chilies with a funky old kitchen knife.

He took his time dicing the chilies and onions ever so small, careful so no one would get a big disagreeable bite. The ingredients were simple: chilies and tomatoes and onions from his garden. He often planted a summer garden specifically for sarsa makings.

And we put sarsa on most everything. Eggs and beans at breakfast, the bean tortilla roll at lunch, the piece of round steak and fried potatoes for dinner. We put it on potato salad, turkey at Thanksgiving, boiled mostaza—the wild mustard greens my grandmother and I would pick after a good rain. At our house, there was nearly always sarsa on the table.

*M*ission San Antonio de Pala was established in 1816 by Padre Antonio Peyri. It survives as an asistencia in the mission system and continues to minister to an Indian congregation.

Every year, as it has from its inception, the mission hosts a Corpus Christi Fiesta. Traditionally, the fiesta features a pit barbecue dinner.

In the seventies, Sam Powvall of the Pauma Reservation and Dennis Subish of the La Jolla Indian Reservation would take charge of the barbecue. It was an all-night thing. A big pit was dug in the ground behind the mission and filled with sawn oak. The oak would burn down to glowing coals, perfect for long, slow barbecuing.

The beef, usually from one of Subish's steers, would be rubbed with garlic powder, chili powder, salt, and pepper. The spiced meat would be wrapped in muslin or aluminum foil and placed inside potato sacks soaked in water. The sacks would be dropped into the pit, which the men covered, usually with corrugated tin. Then they shoveled dirt on top to make it airtight. You had to check it with a flashlight to be sure no smoke escaped. You wanted it airtight.

After eight hours, in time for the afternoon barbecue, the meat would be removed, sliced, and served. Meat for parties is still cooked that way on the rez. I have a pit in my backyard. Nothing better than meat, still hot from the pit, with beans, potato salad, and sarsa.

So many local foods have mission origins. Tortillas, both corn and flour, are still highly prized. Even today, a girl who can make flour tortillas, thin and round and with the right texture, is considered good marriage material.

Yes, the missions did much wrong to us. But they did one right thing: they introduced us to foods and a way of cooking them as good as any on this planet.

For those who want to learn more about the mission/rancho style of cooking, I highly recommend *California Rancho Cooking* by Jacqueline Higuera McMahan and *California Mission Recipes* by Bess A. Cleveland. The recipes in this essay were extracted from these books.

Fiction

ONE HUNDRED WHITE WOMEN

Some forty years ago, following America's blossoming of flower children, there occurred on the Pala Indian Reservation, and other reservations, a marvel of sorts. White women began showing up in Volkswagen vans, in psychedelic pickups with homemade camper shells, in sporty little cars with convertible tops. They came wearing toe rings and nose rings and dangling turquoise earrings—they came searching for answers.

Some took jobs with Indian legal-aid services, or education centers, or health clinics, harboring high-minded intentions of bettering a downtrodden race. The bravest of them rented rusted Airstream trailers parked in pastures where brush cattle left squishy mines along the path to the outhouse. Others rented houses on the rez. The less courageous found apartments in nearby towns and commuted to the reservations.

These women were unlike the women Indian guys were used to. Indian women stayed in the shade, wearing extra-large T-shirts and jeans, worried the sun might make them darker than they already were. These white women paraded around in jean short-shorts and bandana-print halter tops, showing off long white legs they opted not to shave. Hair often bristled from armpits as well. Trading-post headbands, beaded in dime-store designs, kept their long hair in place. Many sported wire-rimmed granny glasses and Birkenstock sandals.

Even stranger, they spoke in multisyllabic words, asking about discrimination, oppression, cultural deprivation. Some even asked Indian guys to get metaphysical with them.

Most Indian men were clueless about what was happening. They just shrugged and went with the flow. "Hey, white women, go figure."

These women carried beliefs in their backpacks, beliefs about shamanism, about noble savagery, about the four directions, about free love. Most of these women were college educated. They had read *Black Elk Speaks, Bury My Heart at Wounded Knee, Custer Died for Your Sins, A Century of Dishonor, The Feminine Mystique.*

Most Indian women, while not prudes, didn't go in for that free-love baloney. If you wanted sex with an Indian woman, you had to treat her right, buy her tortilla rolls at the fiesta, take her to the drive-in, shake hands with her dad. You couldn't expect to show up at her door with a pocket full of peyote and get some free love. It just didn't work that way.

But the white women came looking for magic. They wanted to get next to an Indian man who could teach them about shape-shifting, about astral travel, about herbal cures, about witchery, about Indian lovemaking.

About as far as most of them got was lessons in Indian lovemaking. Indian men were more than willing to teach them that. "You want a little Indian in you," the men would joke to them. As far as the other stuff went, most Indian men had never heard of it, except maybe to drink a little elderberry tea to soothe an upset stomach. But the rest of it, all the magic the anthropology textbooks talked about, most Indian men couldn't or wouldn't deliver.

But I admired the persistence of these white women. They picked up on Indian cadences of speech, the way of drawing out words with a singsong quality. Something wasn't just over there, it was "waaaaaay over there." But they never quite got it right, and we laughed to hear a blonde braless girl in a white tank top talking almost like an Indian—"haaaahhhhh," she'd say. Even blindfolded, you knew it wasn't an Indian talking. And they became known as "wannabes," as in they wanted to be Indian.

Oh, they tried to educate the Indians. Teach the Indians some of their New Age philosophies. More than one Indian man was given a healing crystal he had to wear on a leather thong around his neck. If you saw an Indian brother wearing one of those, you knew he'd been with a white woman.

One white woman, a legend of sorts, arrived midsummer in a white, wobbly-wheeled Volkswagen Bug. Tie-dyed T-shirts served as seat covers. A shriveled-up orange riddled with cloves served as a deodorizer. The car needed deodorizer, for the woman, in her quest to be totally natural, got a little ripe. She also traveled with a black Labrador retriever named Sweetpea, so old most of his teeth had fallen out, so old he smelled of decay, so old he sometimes forgot himself and pissed on the backseat. So the orange-clove deodorizer was welcome.

She went by the name of Feather, but her real name was MaryAnn. Some said she hailed from money and that she was testing her wings. A spoiled girl gone wild.

She rented a one-bedroom house on the reservation, a thin-walled shack with an outhouse out back. In the summer, with no insulation, no breeze coming through the open window, she soaked her old-man's T-shirt with ice water, so her headlights were on high beam. Young Indian boys could be found hanging around her front yard, pitching pennies and looking through her window, hoping for a bit of titillation.

She took up with an Indian guy, a guy who was pretty worthless to begin with. While she went to work, he sat around and drank up the beer she bought. She tried to fit in, but the Indian women mostly gave her refrigerated looks when she said hello.

Feather lasted about six months on the reservation, then got sick of buying her boyfriend's beer. One day, she loaded up Sweetpea and headed out, maybe back to Texas, never to be seen or heard from again.

*Y*es, we made fun. And we shouldn't have. She was like many others—good-hearted women who just didn't understand they were culturally out of their depths. They introduced new ways of thinking to us as well. They tried rez life, and several actually stayed on and are still here. But most came mispronouncing the word *tortilla,* and left a little disillusioned. Sometimes with a little Indian in them.

INDIAN LOVE

The San Ignacio Indian Reservation isn't on a map. It's a dream, a fiction, a nostalgia, a metaphor.

But in many ways, San Ignacio, or San Iggy, as some like to call it, represents many Southern California Indian reservations, and by extension much of Indian Country.

This being SoCal, San Ignacio winters aren't so harsh, more like suggestions, and spring tiptoes in on squirrel feet. Dead leaves, soggy from morning dew, carpet the ground, but new leaves sprout green on winter-bare sycamores—you can feel rebirth.

Fruit trees blossom pink and white in the yard next to the potential classic he promises to restore someday, but that today rusts on cinder blocks. And folks who walk into their yards groan at the ugly inevitability of weeds, the bane of rez life, knowing that many hours at the wrong end of a grubbing hoe are in store. And you think maybe it's time to finally break down and buy that weed whacker you've lusted after.

Spring bursts electric onto the rez. Butterflies wriggle free of cocoons, cottontails emerge from winter dens blinking in the sunlight, Indian women take more time and care in shaving their legs and scraping their heels.

Old, grizzled, battle-scarred rez dogs get a little frisky when a slender, shy pointer saunters by. Young guns wear slingshot T-shirts while playing basketball on the outdoor courts. Teen girls, cat-eyed and petulant, pretty as any God put on this earth, walk by the game, giggly and whispery, their young hips learning about fluidity. In their presence, jump shots get a little higher, the drive to the basket a little more determined, the blocked shot batted away with more oomph.

You know spring is in full bloom when wild lilac turns hillsides purple, and the scent is headier than any perfume shop. Spring causes men in T-shirts to suck in their guts as they walk into the rez store—just in case. Women exchange winter sweats for tight jeans, shorts, or even, for a brave few, yoga pants.

The ball fields, quiet for most of winter, resume activities, and kids chewing wads of bubblegum swing at balls thrown by patient coaches. Adults, too, have oiled their mitts after a winter in the closet, and turn out for pick-up games during the day. They play coed for fun, and linger in the parking lot as dusk turns to night.

Funny how, after the games, the bed of a pickup truck, loaded with an ice chest of beer, becomes such an aphrodisiac. The ball fields go dark and the stars shine white. The night air turns sultry, Pacific breezes carry whiffs of eucalyptus, the love potions kick in. The players, men and women, lean on truck beds to talk and laugh and tease. Eyes meet across the bed, conversations without words occur, women become a little more animated, quicker to laugh; men unnecessarily flex muscles when reaching for a beer.

In the seventies, eight-tracks played George Jones, Fats Domino, and Etta James through tinny speakers. Today iPods are plugged into fancy car stereos, and the young have a different music, a lot of rapping going on, but amid the hip-hop and thump you'll still find a good stash of oldies. These newer generations have grown up with *I Found My Thrill on Blueberry Hill* via parents and grandparents, and teen girls still learn to two-step from dads and granddads.

In the old days, the truck cab might smell of brilliantine, Old Spice, and Marlboros. These days car interiors might smell of store-bought air freshener, Axe body spray, and vape lingerings.

As the night progresses, it's not unheard of for couples to peel away from truck beds to wander off for a time on their lonesome, maybe to explore each other's lips behind a cactus stand and give vent to shared feelings. It is, after all, spring, and love is in the air.

Teenagers meet each other on corners to walk dirt reservation roads, hand in hand. Grandmother Moon ascends, white as a hen's egg nesting in clouds. Moonglow lights the way, illuminating her skin, dancing in her eyes.

But as they pass the cemetery, she picks up the pace and squeezes his hand a little tighter, because you just never know which spirits are about. Once past graves, the talk is low and slow; she's dreaming of college, maybe being a teacher someday. He talks of signing up, being a soldier, like his dad and his granddad. But their talk of leaving the rez and consequently leaving each other is countered by the warmth and fit of each other's hands, and with each step, with each word, with each laugh, it gets harder to let go.

In spring men uncover the backyard barbecues. The more fastidious might even scrape off last year's greasy grit. The charcoal is lit and carne asada sears on the grill. The picnic table brims with fresh guacamole, beans boiled with ham hocks, salsas, both red and green, Indian potato salad made with generous dollops of Best Foods mayonnaise, and a stack of torts. Beers cool in a tub of ice, and people laugh and talk between bites. Dwight Yoakam is on the stereo singing about the pocket of a clown; heads bob as folks chew. After the meal, horseshoes resumes, iron shoes clanging against steel pegs. Men hoot and trash talk when a double ringer is thrown, but these days, more women throw shoes as well, and maybe she tosses the double ringer and trash talk commences in a higher pitch.

In spring a newlywed bride, who takes her new-wife role seriously, is a Native man's dream. She looks terrific barefoot, in bun-hugging shorts and a tight halter top. She's elbow deep in a bowl of dough, her inexperienced fingers trying to hear what her DNA is telling her. Her mother and grandmothers have done this to perfection; she wonders why she didn't pay more attention when they tried to teach her the right consistency for tortilla dough.

But she tries. In her palms, she forms lopsided balls about the size of lemons. She flours the board, pressing out the dough with her rolling pin, flattening it into circles that more closely resemble maps of Texas.

She heats the comal, the cast-iron one she got as a wedding present, and blisters tortillas on it. When cooked, she sets them in a bowl covered with a dish towel. When he comes home from a day of pounding nails to find his wife making tortillas, he smiles big. She looks so cute with bits of dough and flour on her cheek because she tried to swipe hair from her eyes with fingers sticky with dough.

She proudly butters one and hands it to him to sample. And if he knows what's good for him, he won't say a thing about Texas, or how they are a little salty for his taste. No, he'll shut up and eat, making only sounds of pleasure, lavishing her with praise, because when an Indian woman's feelings get hurt there's hell to pay. She may get mad and never make him another tortilla. An Indian marriage without tortillas? Well, let's just say he doesn't want that.

In the fifties and sixties, reservation house parties were Lucky Lager gatherings, that being the Indian beer back then. Tall cans of Lucky Lager would sit everywhere, and whoever cleaned up in the morning would find many half full, but with cigarette butts in them.

And people would stack 45s on the record changer, and the song would go from a bopping "Rock around the Clock," to a grinder from the Platters, to the Stroll, where people would line up and a couple would stroll down the center.

There was something permanent to the Stroll, because there are Indian couples who strolled in 1957 that still stroll today. You see them at Indian weddings, these days grayer, slower, a little rounder, but still able to smile at each other as they dance. And when the wedding is over, they walk out arm in arm, still in love after all these years.

The couple getting married would do well to watch and learn. Because Indian love has its vicissitudes, its good days and bad, days when she thinks her lover no better than a rez dog. But somewhere, deep down, Indian love abides.

Indian love is often a die-hard love, a love spiced with equal parts laughter and passion, and jealousy and contention. But through it all, love can and does endure.

It's a love often begun in the spring, when basketballs swish through nets, and the girls, pretty as all get out, throw cat-eyed glances at the guys, who might try but can't stop thinking about them.

THE RING-CARD GIRL

She has long legs of high-heeled invitation, can-can legs that go from here to there. Long black hair, adorned by a beaded eagle feather, teases the thunderbird tattooed at the small of her back. Silver-feather earrings dangle; silver necklaces wrap her neck. Silver glitter flecks rouged cheeks. She adjusts the chamois bikini top, hitches up the straps of the thong to align high on her hips. The ring attendant nods: Ready? She nods back. She's up next.

The timekeeper, a couple of chairs away, pounds his palm against the canvas, slapping off ten seconds to go, then clangs the bell ending the round. Good thing, because an overmatched Mexican middleweight is getting rocked by a tall, whip-fast black fighter. The beaten man needs a breather. Etta stands, her butt cheeks sticking to the orange plastic chair. She takes an unsteady first step in spiky high heels. She'd have preferred bare feet, but the heels are part of the job. One bonus, the high angle defines her calf muscles; she likes the slinky result. She climbs a stepladder to snake through vinyl-covered ropes, her hind end jutting out to the thrill of ringsiders. Some whistle. Some moan lasciviously. Some bay like hound dogs.

She dodges the bloodied fighter who can't find his corner and grabs the ROUND 5 placard from the wide-mouthed ring attendant who Etta thinks looks like Martha Raye in a toupee. She hoists the card overhead, putting her girls on parade. She fixes a cheerleader smile, inhales sharply to give her abdomen the desired flatness, and steps—no, strides—around the ring, leggy and lush, hips grinding like a stripper's.

Her skin is all sheen under hot television lights. Time inside the ring feels otherworldly—slow and heavenly. Faceless men, sloshing beer in plastic cups, whistle and hoot with upraised fists as she struts by. She looks good. She works hard to look good. Pilates three nights a week, jogging every morning, weight training every other morning, nothing to eat after 6:00 p.m. Feline-quick muscles rippling beneath coppery skin. Men climb on seats to get her attention, waving arms, whistling. She puckers glossy red lips and blows air kisses, smiling a bleached-tooth smile. Was this how Marilyn Monroe felt?

She thought she'd hate the slobbery attention of fight fans, the leers and guttural come-ons from a drunken herd. But this is her fourth fight, and rather than dreading it, she digs the hoopla. Her cousin Moe, who sits on the gaming commission for San Ignacio's Two Suns Casino, urged that she try the ring-card gig. "You're a natural," he said.

Initially, she'd balked at the idea of jiggling in nothing but a thong bikini for strangers. But the TV cameras occasionally focused on ring-card girls, and that was national exposure. Her new motto: "Early to bed, early to rise, work like hell, and advertise." And you never knew. You just never knew what might come of getting your face and, let's face it, your body out there.

Besides, she's been a lifelong boxing fan. She grew up watching TV fights with her grandfather, sitting on the afghan-covered couch, her skinny leg touching his big leg, both eating cheese quesadillas, him sipping longneck beer, her drinking Pepsi from a Tupperware cup. As a youth, her grandfather boxed Golden Gloves, and he never quite left the ring. During TV fights, he bobbed and weaved in his chair, explaining the different punches and strategies to her. So she understands the boxing vocabulary; she thrills to a well-thrown hook. The ring-card thing is working out. She makes three hundred dollars a night plus tips, gets a ringside seat for matches, some of them big-name fighters, and, not the least of it, she gets attention. She notices how the crowd exhales disappointment when her ring stroll ends. She feels desired.

"Boy, you're making them drool tonight," says Syn, the methamphetamine-lean ring-card girl seated next to Etta.

"Ah, they're all faced. They'd hoot at a bag lady," Etta says, a little breathless, as she returns to her seat.

The bell rings; the fighters clash again in the middle of the ring. The Mexican fighter, either too proud or too stunned, won't clinch the opponent. Etta wishes he would. He just keeps eating leather. Her cell phone fires off in the small purse at her feet. She rolls her eyes and looks at Syn.

"You gonna answer it?" Syn asks.

"I guess."

She picks up the phone and sees the displayed number. She catches Syn's glance and sighs.

"Hello," she says. She almost shouts into the phone to be heard above the crowd. A bit of her blood-red lipstick smears the screen as she talks.

"Hey, babe," Snazz says. "Wuss up?" She hears the beer in his bravado, his uncalled-for animation.

"I'm working."

"I can hear. Are ya gonna be finished soon? I miss you."

"Who knows? We're in the fifth, but you know how fights are."

"Yeah, yeah. But hurry home 'kay? And could you stop at the

mini-mart and pick me up a twelver?"

So that's why he's calling. "You drank all that beer already?"

"Calvin came over and had a few. Plus, I'm a thirsty boy."

Great, now I'm buying Calvin beer too, she thinks. "Whatever. I gotta go."

"Bye-bye, baby. I'll be here just being your ever-lovin' man."

She ends the call without saying goodbye.

"What you gonna do?" Syn asks.

"I dunno." Etta shoves the phone into her purse, lifts a stick of gum from an opened pack, unwraps it with shiny red fingernails, folds it, sticks it into her mouth.

Her mother warned her that chewing gum was a low-class habit. Her mother, yeah, who once got sick from drinking aftershave.

Her mother's favorite singer was Etta James, the great blues vocalist. Etta has never cared much for the name, but she does like the singer. A flashier name might be good, though, and she toys with changing it. She's always liked Sacheen, like Sacheen Littlefeather, the Indian woman made famous by standing in for Marlon Brando at the Academy Awards. She went to the library and looked up Sacheen's seventies spread in *Playboy* magazine after hearing about it. Etta knew many Natives questioned Sacheen's standing as an activist, but Etta admires her style.

When Etta was a sophomore in high school, a guidance counselor, a gray-haired out-of-state Indian woman named Mrs. Luckwater, told Etta she thought Indians with talent had an obligation to work hard, to make the best of themselves to help raise up the people. If more Indians saw other Indians getting successful in the arts, in business, in science, in anything besides sitting on the rez drinking themselves into diabetes and bad livers, all Indian people might benefit. Indian kids would see there is more to life than getting high. Etta believed that. She works every day toward success. She doesn't do it for money or fame. She strives to be a Luiseño woman other Indians, especially kids, can look up to. A strong Indian woman who lives a balanced, productive life. If fame is a by-product of that, so be it. A small measure of fame might help her to make a bigger impact.

Although undecided about her future career, she leans toward the creative side, taking photography and art classes at California State University, San Marcos. She has in mind doing a residency at an American Indian arts institute in Santa Fe, so she is studying the photography greats—especially women photographers: Dorthea Lange, Imogen Cunningham, Margaret Bourke-White, Annie Leibovitz. She is also into film. She analyzes François Truffaut films, frame by frame in the media room, absorbing how he set up shots. She auditions for every student play and recently performed the Elizabeth Taylor role in *Who's Afraid of Virginia Woolf?* And she nailed it, dammit. She did. She can act.

She doesn't want to rely on looks for success. Over time, looks wither. She wants to create beauty, not just flash some skin. She pursues the theory behind the art. Hell, she even read Aristotle's *Poetics* to learn the structure of art from the ground up. She envisions herself at the helm of a huge movie camera someday, making films that will not just entertain but open eyes and break down stereotypes.

But, too, she likes being in front of an audience. When she was five years old, just a gap-toothed, skinny girl in thrift-store tap shoes, she danced in front of their Christmas tree, her aunts, uncles, and grandparents clapping for her, dropping coins into a gray felt cowboy hat she set atop a TV tray. While she shuffle-ball-stepped to "Tea for Two," she bubbled with emotion, and the universe threw its arms around her and hugged her tight. Her cheeks flushed with the warmth of being liked. To this day, those feelings of acceptance fuel her ambitions.

Snazz, her husband, runs contrary to her ambitions. He sits at home, day after day, smoking dope, drinking beer, grooving to reggae, watching TV. No dreams. No thoughts of tomorrow. Just another stick of furniture in her trailer. Except she has to feed this furniture, and at 280 pounds, Snazz has slapped on 60 pounds of cushioning in three years.

Etta sits with her knees together, her hands folded. She pops and snaps her Doublemint gum—a noisy habit, her mom would say. As she watches, the fighter with the bloodied eye and the bloodied yellow satin trunks takes a crushing double left hook—first to the body, then to the jaw. He plops on the canvas like overcooked spaghetti. The ref counts him out and, just like that, Fight Night is over.

Etta waits for a moment, watching the Mexican fighter sprawled too still on the canvas. Is he okay? He's stretched out, arms and legs in the shape of a cross, blood pooling from his gashed eyebrow. The ring physician, a gray-templed man in a tweed coat, hurries to him, checking his eyes with a Maglite, then waves smelling salts under his nose. The fighter's red high-tops jerk as he returns to consciousness. Etta breathes easier. She enjoys the sport, the artistry and the bravery of it, but she doesn't want anyone to get seriously jacked up. Etta herself has done some boxing and considered turning pro, but knockouts like that dissuaded her. Etta has been hit before. She didn't like it. It hurt.

Ready to leave, she slips into a white satin boxing robe, leaving it untied, peekaboo-style. Still on display, still in ring-card girl character, she and Syn seduce along the aisle toward the back dressing room. Men, and even some women, congratulate them on a good show. "You girls were awesome, better than the fight," says one twenty-something in muttonchops and a black leather jacket.

A drunk guy, shaved head, handlebar mustache, coiled cobras

tattooed on his thick arms, paws Etta's ass as she passes by. He palms her butt cheek, squeezing.

"Hey, hey, Pocahontas," he says with a leer.

She clenches in response.

Anger rises like lava. She doesn't think, doesn't weigh pros and cons; she just reacts. She wheels, steady as she can in her high heels, and slugs the guy in the face with a tight fist.

"What the hell do you think you're doing, you bastard?" Etta hisses, a bobcat pitched for a scrap.

Her knuckles bust his lip and send him reeling backward. He slops foamy beer down the front of his T-shirt. His eyes bug; he bellows with the flash of pain.

Two guys in security jackets, earphones wired into their ears, microphones clipped to their lapels, descend on the scene in seconds.

"What's going on here?" asks Larry, a wide-shouldered, four-hundred-pound security guard in a blue sport coat and gray slacks. Larry is from San Ignacio. He lives down the road from Etta.

"This sonofabitch grabbed my ass, Larry, so I socked him," Etta says through her teeth.

Why does it have to be like this? Why does she have to fight at every turn just to get some respect? All her life, man, all her days growing up, pinched and prodded by assholes. And she feels ready to kill the next bastard who calls her Pocahontas. Was that the only Indian woman white people had ever heard of?

"He did, Larry, he did grab her ass," Syn says.

"Sir, would you come with me, please?"

"What? No way. She hit me. That bitch hit meeee," the guy yells, pounding his chest. He lowers his hand from his mouth, and blood drips from the swollen cut. He definitely has a fat lip.

"Sir, did you touch the lady?" Larry asks.

"I was getting outta my seat and I may have brushed against…"

"Larry, he grabbed me. Pure and simple," Etta says.

"He did. I saw him," Syn says.

"Sir, I know this woman. She wouldn't hit you for no reason. We have a witness, it's on videotape..."

"Just like you goddamn Indians. You all stick up for each other. I'm getting out of this shithole and I ain't never coming back."

"That, sir, would be best for all," Larry says.

The man hulks off, flipping the bird in stride.

"Sorry, Etta," Larry says. "The guy's a jerk-off."

"I'm cool," Etta says, still breathing hard.

"But please, Etta, stop hitting people in here. It's bad for the ring-card-girl image," Larry says, smiling.

"I know, I know, but I can't stand it when men pull that crap."

"Later, Etta," Larry says, touching her shoulder in a gesture of support. "Behave yourself."

Etta and Syn continue their walk to the dressing room, Etta rubbing the sore spot on her knuckles. To act in violence rankles her, upsets her stomach, makes her shaky. But sometimes she just lashes out. When cornered, she fights. She can't help herself.

*E*tta heads for the bar. She isn't much of a drinker. She'd seen her mother plowed—face like melted wax, mouth slack-jawed, pants pissed—too many times to want it for herself. But on Fight Nights she allows herself two gin and tonics.

She finds two empty stools at the Indian side of the bar and saves one for Syn. Etta revels in the celebritydom of the moment, people casting looks, strangers pointing her out. Once a guy asked her to autograph a cocktail napkin. Others send her drinks. Often she has to turn down men, some of them pretty dang good-looking too, asking for dates. She just smiles, shakes her head no, and points at the small diamond on her ring finger. "Sorry, married," she says.

But while she can, Etta basks in the glow. The fans make her feel desired, accepted, like she's more than a half-educated, fatherless daughter of a drunk mother. Hell, Etta grew up on commodity cheese, had eaten boiled rice and powdered milk for dinner when there was nothing else. Stop thinking that way, Etta tells herself. Or for sure, this night'll turn into a pity party.

Syn walks up after a few minutes, her stringy blonde hair damp at the edges. She has splashed her face with cold water and freshened her makeup. Pink gloss glistens her lips. Light freckles pepper her nose. Redness from a stinging hit of meth rims her dilated amber eyes. She's twenty-one, same as Etta, but looks thirty. Her skin, dull and grainy under the makeup, has endured too many sleepless nights. But if you don't look too close, she's a looker. Blonde and busty, not hippy, and long-legged like a Vegas showgirl.

Syn sucks on a Virginia Slim as she lowers herself onto the stool next to Etta. Etta and Syn are loose friends, even phone each other a couple of times a week between fights. Workdays, Syn studies for her realtor's license. But Etta has noticed in the short time they've known each other that her meth use has increased. Not good, Etta thinks. Syn is indeed humming tonight.

"Some guy just tipped me twenty bucks as I was walking out," Syn says, her eyes bulging with drug-induced astonishment.

"Syn, what did you do? You didn't do anything, did you?"

"If you're thinking I gave this guy a hand job for twenty bucks, you're smokin' crack."

"They'll kick you out of here for that. They have cameras everywhere."

"I didn't do nothing. He just walked up to me, handed me a twenty, and said thanks for making his night. So I'm buying. Whaddya want?"

"T&T, extra lime," Etta tells the bartender who moved in for their order. Syn orders a margarita on the rocks for herself.

"So are you going home tonight?" Syn asks.

"I guess so."

"Will he be home?"

"You heard him. He wants me to bring him beer."

"Are you going to say anything to him?"

"I guess so. Probably. I don't know."

"Christ, what will you say?"

"I'm still working on that."

The bartender, a tall, ruddy surfer dude in a white shirt and a black bow tie, hands the girls their drinks.

Syn pays him and leaves a two-dollar tip. "He's cute," Syn says.

"Syn, you promised."

"Come on, girlfriend, I gotta do something to live up to my name."

"You should change that name. What's your real name anyway?"

"Priscilla. How boring is that?"

A jazz trio—piano, stand-up bass, and drums—slinks through a version of Van Morrison's "Moondance" on a stage behind the bar. The piano player, a black woman in a colorful African dress, sings the words in a husky voice.

A labyrinth of video slot machines buzzes and dings and flashes colored lights behind the girls. Casino people stream behind them, some laughing, some walking hand in hand, some solo, staring blank-eyed with the horror of heavy losses.

"I guess you gotta tell him," Syn says, stirring her margarita with her finger, licking her finger, then taking a sip.

"Yeah," Etta says. "It's getting so I hate going home. I can't take it anymore."

"Least you don't have any kids."

Tendons in Etta's jaw tense. She jostles her drink in her pinched grip, ice cubes clinking too loudly in the tall glass. She sighs, her shoulders droop. She sips, shuddering at the gin's juniper bite.

Etta had married Snazz three years earlier, when she was eighteen. She married him after she'd found herself pregnant. She wasn't sure how she'd let it happen. She must have forgotten to take her pill. Must have, because usually she was careful as hell. She was frantic at first. She imagined stretch marks on her huge belly. She shuddered at the thought of 3:00 a.m. feedings, the baby collapsing her breasts with excessive suction, of looking for babysitters on school days. She might even have to drop out, and she had just started college. A baby would surely explode her dreams. But several weeks went by and she discovered a warming love for the new life growing in her womb. Instead of agonized visions of child-rearing, she pictured rocking the baby to sleep in her grandmother's rocking chair. She felt the tiny fingers grasp her fingers, the way she'd felt other babies do. She began to see herself pushing a stroller, her baby in a bonnet, and the reservation women stopping her to see the infant. "Oooh," they'd coo, and pinch chubby cheeks. And this would be her baby, her flesh and blood, her genes, her appreciations, her apprehensions, her bundle of dreams.

And Snazz talked about fatherhood with an awed tone of voice, about playing catch with his son, about teaching the boy to shoot a .22, about turning wrenches and tuning the Camaro. If it was a daughter, he'd say, that'd be okay, too. He'd teach her to play softball and shoot hoops. He'd take her to piano lessons. He'd be a good father, he promised. And Etta bought into his daydreams. She wanted to believe. They married quickly in the San Ignacio Mission, the Italian priest pronouncing their vows. A Mexican band with a hot horn section played cumbias, rancheras, and salsas at the reception in the tribal hall, and the people danced. Even her mother behaved herself, getting just giddily tight.

Snazz looked sharp in his tux. He had the fastest Camaro on the reservation. And they had known each other all their lives. As kids, on hot summer days, they'd tossed water balloons at each other. When a water balloon doused her shirt, he joked about her budding headlights. And the teasing made her nipples tingle. Snazz was a good athlete, the class clown, a nice guy. And in those days, there was something comforting about Snazz. He was kind. Etta believed Snazz loved her. Knew it in her marrow.

Shortly after the wedding, as she pinned laundry on the backyard clothesline, a violent cramp twisted up her womb. Her insides felt ready to burst, the way a water balloon bursts. She grimaced in panic, fear broiling deep in her interior. She dashed for the bathroom, and the second she hit the toilet seat, she doubled over. Her insides gushed, splashing blood and tissue against the porcelain bowl. What was happening? But she had a notion. Primal instinct told her she was losing her child.

Her pale lips curled into a mournful cry, almost a wolf's howl. She wailed with an ache of emptiness that welled up from her womb. She stood, delirious with pain, to plunge her hand into the bloody toilet bowl, feeling around until she touched with her fingertips the glob she sought. It hurt too much to look at. What if she saw a tiny face? What if she saw tiny hands? She couldn't bear that. Nor could she bear to just flush the fetus into the sewer, like it was a turd or something. She went to her drawer for a blue bandana to wrap the baby, no bigger than a golf ball. She wrapped by feel, not looking. When done, she crumbled to the floor and moaned over all the things that wouldn't happen, all the cuddling and soothing and closeness she would miss. Her baby, real to her as if it had been a living, breathing presence, was dead. The fetus was maybe two months old, too young for a funeral. But Snazz dug a hole next to her grandmother's grave, and she placed the bundle into her grandmother's embrace.

"Watch over her, Grandmother," she prayed, to both her real grandmother and Grandmother Moon. She didn't know if the baby was a girl, but it felt feminine, so she identified it so. "She's my girl. That makes her your girl, too. Please, Grandmother, be good to her. The way you were good to me."

Snazz's eyes spilled tears too, his rubbery lips sinking into the forlorn. No gootchy-gootchy-goo, no "Rock-a-bye Baby," no infant falling asleep on the chest. But something, besides the baby, died that day. Something deflated, at least for her, and their bond of love no longer held air. The baby had given their union purpose; without the baby, their being together felt empty, nothing more than a pretense.

"Do you love him?" Syn asks. Syn's question jolts Etta from her reverie. Suddenly, the noise and mayhem of the casino go mute for Etta. The rowdies at the other end of the bar blur. For the thousandth time, she rummages through her insides, lifting under floor mats and pulling back curtains, seeking love for Snazz. She finds friendliness for Snazz, and in many ways pity. But romantic love? None there.

"Naw, I don't love him. That's the thing. I don't love him. It's like I feel more sorry for him than anything. Sometimes I wonder if maybe I'm transferring some of the feelings I had for our baby onto him."

"You had a baby?" Syn asks, shocked. No stretch marks, no sign of pregnancy on her flawless abdomen.

"I had a baby. But I had a miscarriage. It ripped my heart out," Etta says.

"So sorry, Etta. Geez, that must have been tough." Syn's meth-revved eyes dart about.

"Tough? Yeah. You could say that," Etta says, in understatement. With that, she gulps her drink, gin burning her throat.

"I loved my baby."

Syn lays a hand on Etta's trembling shoulder.

Etta, with mascara about to bleed: "My mother's only words of advice to me were 'Don't have kids, Etta, don't have kids.' She told me that one morning when I was sixteen and she was going through the trash, looking for a corner left in a vodka bottle to quiet her shakes."

"Whoa, that's harsh," Syn says.

"I know; I'm a mess. Try as I do, I just can't seem to love Snazz. I know he loves me...What's not to love?" she says, trying to joke through tears. "But love can't be one-sided. I'm beginning to wonder if I need a shrink," Etta says.

Part of the problem, Etta is sure, is that he has become some kind of wannabe Rastafarian. This dope-smoking, "it's all good bro" kind of guy who has no vision, no drive, no thoughts of anything bigger. Oh, he talks of world peace but can't even muster himself to the polls to vote in a presidential election. Etta hates to admit it, but she sees him as weak. No character. No follow-through. "If a thing is worth starting, it's worth finishing. Never quit, Etta, never give up," her grandfather used to tell her. But Snazz is a quitter. She has lost all respect for him. Is lethargy grounds for divorce?

Sex had devolved into this once-a-month ordeal of being smashed and smothered by his excess. When they were young, before the weight, before the loss of their child, Etta enjoyed sex with Snazz. She even screamed out with the occasional orgasm. But sex these days had gone flat, a glass of Pepsi left overnight on the nightstand.

Each morning, she rises early to face the East for the ritual greeting of the sun, but these days it is with a groan. She has to get out of this dead end. She has to tell him.

Coming home from the casino, her SUV slashes through puddles in the dirt road leading to her trailer. She thinks of it as her trailer, not their trailer. She writes the checks for it, after all. A small spotted frog jumps into headlight brightness, then disappears beneath her front bumper. She hopes it didn't get squished beneath her off-road tires. The rain brings them out, she thinks. She glances in her rearview mirror but sees no sign of the frog.

Boo, her German shepherd, crawls out from under the wooden porch as she pulls up. He barks once, then recognizes her Toyota 4Runner and stands waiting, tail wagging. As she pulls on the door handle to get out, exhaustion hits her. She needs a hot bath and bed. But she's bracing for a long, emotional night.

She grabs the Bud twelve-pack off the passenger seat and steps out, her Uggs digging into the damp driveway gravel. Wet cactus and sage scent the night. A stand of cottonwood trees claws at the starry sky with leafless branches. Boo wriggles over, boisterous-eyed, his whole back end a dance, his warm breath exhaling vapors in the crisp air. She pats his thick-boned head; he licks her hand. He wants to—but doesn't—jump on her. She broke him of that.

She kicks her SUV door closed and gazes into the black sky, grasping at anything to forestall going in. The rain has cleared. A sliver of moon, like a clipped thumbnail, floats bright amid the stars. She stills herself, for a moment, in reverence for her ancestors. It's her Luiseño belief that the souls of the dead are transformed into stars after a three-day journey heavenward. The stars twinkle in friendly greeting. Three times she grunts, her traditional acknowledgment of respect. She singles out the star she calls Grandfather; one next to it, Grandmother—in her mind and in her heart she hugs them both, rejoicing that they continue in beauty, their lives forever in the present tense.

She looks one last time at the firmament, beseeching the help of all her ancestors. She feels old as the stars, tired as faded light. One by one, she trudges up the porch steps; thin boards complain with her weight. She opens the front door to enter unhappiness. She shivers in the claustrophobia of it. No porch light on. No kitchen light on. Nothing to welcome her but the glow of the TV in the living room, the volume too loud. She sets the twelve-pack on the kitchen counter, unzips her hooded sweatshirt, and drapes it over the back of a kitchen chair. She hesitates a moment. He's more than likely pasted to the recliner. Heartburn heats her stomach. She swallows back the acid. She tightens her abdomen, knowing what must come. Down the short hall into the living room, girls on trampolines jump, spreading their legs on the TV. He's watching *The Man Show*, a salute to the lowest common denominator in males.

She can't see him in the high-backed recliner. Building steam, she marches over to the TV to mute the volume, without looking back at him. She has things to say. She expects his protests, but nothing happens. His chair, the leather recliner she bought at Jerome's for the house, is empty.

Her stomach lurches. "Snazz?" she calls out.

The dark trailer sounds dead except for a creak, one of the unaccountable noises mobile homes make as they settle.

"Snazz," she calls again. Her voice echoes. Must be in the bathroom. He spends a lot of time in there. She heads to the bathroom but sees no light beneath the door. She knocks. "Snazz? You in there?" No sound, except for the blood rushing to her head. She tries the knob. It turns. She pushes the door open, flips up the silent light switch. Not there.

She tries the bathroom in their bedroom. Light breaks through the half-open door. He must be in there. She shoves the door. "Snazz!"

Shirtless on the bathroom linoleum, long black dreadlocks fanned across the fat of his back, dead still.

"Jesus," Etta says, kneeling by his side, feeling for a pulse in his neck, the way she learned in first-aid class.

His skin is warm. Then she spots the slightest quiver in his love handles. He can't hold it any longer—he busts out laughing.

"Psych!" he says, continuing to laugh as he rises to one elbow.

For a moment, anger chokes Etta's words, clamps her throat shut. She gapes in disbelief. What possible kick could he derive from this bullshit prank? What kind of infant was he?

Etta backs away. In a voice curt with forced calm, she says, "Get off the floor, Snazz."

"Aw, come on, baby, don't get mad. I just be playin'," he says, lumbering to his feet. "I heard you pull in. I thought we'd have some fun." Several snarls of Snazz's hair, his lion's mane, as he likes to say, fall into his face, and his eyes take on that sad puppy-dog expression, the one that works so well for him.

Much as she doesn't want to, Etta starts crying.

"Oh, baby, I'm okay. No need to cry," he says.

He stands before her, shoeless, toenails unclipped, jeans hanging low beneath the overhang of his gut. She spends hour after gut-busting hour in the gym to come home to this?

She levels her eyes, the way a marksman levels a target rifle. "You know, in all the time we've been together," she says, no longer crying, "I've never seen you read a book."

Snazz's eyes simper in confusion. "What?"

"I've never seen you read a book."

Etta catches herself in the bathroom mirror. She can see Snazz, too. We are an impossible-looking couple, she thinks. Her focus shifts and she notices flecks of food on the mirror from his flossing. Get me out of this nightmare.

"No, baby, you're the reader in the family," he says.

"Snazz, I can't live with you anymore."

"You can't live with me?"

"No, Snazz."

"What are you talking about?" Snazz's face goes blank, his eyebrows furrow with confusion. He shakes his head, at a loss.

"We're on two different paths. I work. I go to school. I dream of bigger things. You, you do nothing."

"Let's get out of the bathroom, baby, and go sit down. I can see you've got things on your mind."

Snazz walks past her into the living room, takes his place in the recliner. Etta sits on the couch to his left.

"I want a divorce, Snazz." Etta doesn't equivocate. She drills into his eyes, never flinching.

"Tell me again, why?"

Snazz can't abide the intensity of her stare. He shifts his gaze toward the sliding glass door, the one that leads out to the porch he said he'd build but never did.

"Look at me, Snazz. LOOK AT ME!" Etta says.

Snazz's head rotates in her direction, but he still avoids her eyes.

"I don't love you," she says.

"How can you say that? You're my soul mate."

She looks at this bear cub of a boy, his hair matted against his face, his bitch tits sagging onto his belly. She can smell the marijuana odors in the house, after she had asked him not to smoke in here.

"But you're not MY soul mate," she says.

"But why, baby, why? You at least gotta tell me why?" He pleads to know why, like a whiny kid whose mother tells him he can't go to the movies.

"You don't do anything. You don't do a goddamn thing, and I'm sick of it."

"You think I do nothing? I pray all day. I pray for world peace. I pray for a clean heart. I pray for a better world. I pray for you. I pray for me."

"Are you kidding me? All you do is smoke dope all day."

"There is prayer in ganja," he says. "There is prayer in the music I listen to. It's all about peace and love, baby. Peace and love."

"Is there peace and love in Bud? And who's paying for this peace and love bullshit? Who? I am. I'm paying the bills."

"I missed being enrolled by one-sixteenth blood," Snazz says. "A thimbleful more of blood and I'd be getting the casino money, too. It's money given to you. You don't work for it. What's so wrong with sharing with your family? Because I'm your family."

Etta chokes on exasperation. How was she going to get out of this? How?

"I don't want you to be my family, dammit. My family...my baby, is dead. You're nothing to me. Get it? Nothing." Etta's voice teeters between anger and self-pity. "Once you were the father of my baby. But my baby is dead."

"We can make another baby." He uses his gentlest voice, the same voice he used when he talked her into sex in the backseat of his Camaro when they were teenagers. It's a voice she has trouble resisting.

"No, we can't. We won't. Because you're leaving. It's dead between us."

Snazz stands up and, like a soap opera actor, says, "You can keep it alive between us. You can. Besides, baby, I have nowhere to go. This is my—"

"That is not my problem. Now get your shirt on and get out. I'll box up your stuff and send it to you tomorrow."

Then a sideways anger flashes in Snazz's milky eyes. "You know, you probably killed our baby. All your sit-ups, abs of steel bullshit.

You probably shook that baby loose. You killed our baby!" The meanness of his words hits harder than a fist.

"How can you say that to me? How?" cries Etta.

"Baby, I won't leave you. You're my woman for life."

"I'm not your woman. I'm your meal ticket. Get the hell out." Etta's fury escalates.

He picks up a green-glass ashtray and throws it like a football through the window, glass shattering. Pure drama from him. Cold air hits her face.

"You're paying for that window!" she screams.

He screams back, "I ain't paying for shit!"

"Where's all that Rasta peace and love shit now, huh? Fucking poser."

"Shut up and get to bed, Etta." Snazz, stomps his foot, his high school sports trophies rattling in their glass case.

"What? You're ordering me to bed?"

"That's right. Go to bed. We'll talk about this in the morning."

"Are you fucking nuts? You're leaving now or I'm calling the cops."

"Call 'em. I don't give a rat's ass what you do."

She goes around to the table and reaches for the phone in her purse. He runs over, snatches her phone, and throws it against the refrigerator door. The plastic case breaks open as it hits the floor.

He feints like he's going to head-butt her. For the second time that night, she throws a right. This time at his face. The fist pops the side of his jaw. He reels back, his face stricken. Shaking his head clear, his eyes bloodshot and maniacal, he charges. He's too heavy for her to keep him off her. He clenches her throat and squeezes her windpipe. Etta gags at the pressure of his thumbs digging into her neck. Again by instinct, she swings her fist, an uppercut sinking into his belly, but it's like hitting a pillow of lard. It has no effect. The world closes in on her. She is underwater, drowning in an indigo sea. But before she surrenders to darkness, he releases his hands.

"Baby, baby, I don't want this," he says, his voice crumbling with sobs.

Etta, her throat constricted, can't talk. She throws her head back against the refrigerator to open her air passage. The stainless-steel refrigerator door vibrates through her scalp.

Etta swallows for air. His face, broken up, looks devastated, the way it did the day his mother died. Etta remembers his total despair. She was there ten years ago when his mother passed in a back bedroom, her organs collapsing with prolonged diabetes. Etta had provided solace.

"I don't want this," he says, his eyes brimming with tears. "I want you. I don't want this."

Snazz moves in slow motion, like the walking dead. "I didn't cheat on you," he says. "I've been true to you. The only thing I did wrong is love you too much. I can change, baby. I can change. You want me to lose weight. I'll lose weight. You want me to get a job. I'll get a job. Whatever you want, I'll do."

Etta's anger melts. She sees him, like he was when they were twelve and they walked across the swinging bridge laughing and singing Fats Domino songs.

It would be so much easier to give in. To just take him by the hand and lead him to the bedroom. To just make up and forget this night. That's what married couples do, isn't it? They fight, they make up, they stay together. He stands before her, his lower lip quivering like a four-year-old's. She can't shake the image of him as a boy.

Maybe he will change, she thinks. Maybe. But she knows he won't. And she'd have to do this all over again. God, she wants sleep. She says in slow, low volumes, so low he squints to hear, "I'm leaving you Snazz. When I come back tomorrow, I want you to be gone. It's over. You know it's over. You can't kick a dead horse. Just let it go. Just let me go. If you love me, let me go."

"But Et…"

"No, Snazz, no. It's too late. Please be gone tomorrow."

Etta takes her sweatshirt off the back of the chair and heads out the door. She turns for one last time to look at Snazz. He's tearing open the twelve-pack for a can of Bud. She escapes out the front door, looks up at the sky, and doesn't know whether to smile or cry. She feels lighter, though. So much lighter. She wants to cartwheel with relief.

She walks to the 4Runner, her long runner's legs carrying her effortlessly. She opens the door for Boo. He jumps in without questions. She starts the car, turns the wheel to make it out of the circular drive, heading back out the dirt road toward the casino. She'll get a hotel room for a night. And tomorrow will be hers. She's turned the page. If he's not gone, she will call security to bodily remove him. She thinks it should hurt more than it does, to leave her husband, to leave the boy she has known all her life. But she is swimming toward a new shore. From now on, life will be on her terms. She presses the gas pedal a little harder. Should it feel this good to be free?

MAKE MINE RARE

I couldn't see the car through the oleanders, but the engine knock told me it was Harold Owens in his '48 Buick. He braked, and treadbare tires slid in the dirt.

"Hey, Maxie," he called through the open window. "You there?"

"Yeah, come in," I said.

He pushed through the gate butt first, then turned to face me. He was bear-hugging a fifty-pound sack of potatoes. His cheeks puffed. Sweat beaded on his forehead.

"You want some spuds?" he asked.

"Sure," I said. "Set them down anywhere."

Owens, a white guy who lived in Oceanside, seldom had money, but he paid his way on the reservation by stealing produce, then selling or trading it away.

A couple of weeks ago, I had shot a deer, a young forked-horn, up by the granite quarry, and I was boiling stew meat in a cast-iron Dutch oven set into coals in the fire pit outside. It was too damn hot to cook inside.

"You wouldn't happen to have a little taste on hand, would you?" he asked.

He knew damn well I did. He wouldn't have come around otherwise. Owens had a knack for smelling wine even with the lid screwed tight.

"Look in the fridge; there's a bottle in there. May as well bring it out, and I'll have a shot with you," I said.

Owens set the potatoes on the bench in front of my shack and stepped through the homemade screen door. He limped a little. There was still some shrapnel buried near his right knee, a little gift from the Japanese.

He came out and handed me the bottle. I took a drink and offered it back to him. He was polite that way. He wouldn't drink first if it wasn't his bottle.

He took a deep drink of the cold Thunderbird and exhaled pleasure. "Damn, that's good," he said.

"Have another," I said.

"You're twisting my arm."

I unfolded a pocketknife and cut open the potato sack. I removed a couple of good-sized potatoes, quartered them, and dropped them into the stew.

"Stew again?" he asked.

"Yep," I said.

"Don't you ever get tired of stew?"

"Yep," I said.

"Tell you what. It's Friday; Sally Ann gets paid tonight. Why not come over for a real home-cooked meal," he said.

I'd been eating deer meat two weeks straight. The offer tempted.

"Your woman wouldn't care?"

"Hell no. She'd like the company."

I doubted that. I didn't know Sally Ann. Never met her. But I'd never met a working woman who liked strange drunks in her house.

"Sure," he said. "We can eat a good dinner, have some drinks, you can sleep on the couch, and I'll drive you home in the morning."

His brown Buick lumbered through the curves of Highway 76 as it coursed along the willowed banks of the San Luis Rey River, the other potato sacks in the trunk pressing heavy against the springs. Owens shifted into second and the engine kicked up in pitch, knocking ever faster.

"Are we gonna make it?" I asked.

"Oh, hell yes," he said. "She sounds a little rough, but she's got plenty miles left in her."

Owens wore brogans, work boots tied with leather laces that Jimmie Rodgers might have rode trains in. Potato sack dirt smeared his khaki pants. He left his Hawaiian shirt unbuttoned, showing his ginger-haired, freckled chest.

This should tell you a little bit about Owens. He's the only guy I know who'd been bitten twice by rattlesnakes. Both times in the right arm. His arm remained disfigured, bent and shriveled, from the bites.

I catch snakes for fun and profit. Why he wanted one? I have no clue, but he said he had to have it. He was grown man, so I sold him one. I warned him, warned him twice, but did he listen? He sat on my front porch and let it crawl around on his lap. Of course, the snake struck. He's lucky it didn't bite him somewhere else.

You'd think he'd have learned, but a couple years later I was bringing a snake home in a flour sack and he stuck his hand in, trying to see it. Sure as shit, the black diamond bit him. I drove him to the Fallbrook hospital both times.

On our way to Oceanside, where he lived, we pulled into the gravel parking lot of Perry's, the small country store in Bonsall. Owens turned the key, but the engine dieseled for thirty seconds.

"You see, she likes to run so much, you can't hardly shut her down," he said.

Perry, a gray-beard in bib overalls, waved us in. He stood behind a brass turn-of-the-century National Cash Register, his unruly beard stained with tobacco juice.

"Ah, good to see you, gentlemen," he said.

"Say hey, Perry," I said. "How's your bunions?"

"Oh, hell, they been acting up something fierce. I've tried every liniment in the store. 'Bout the only thing that works is Ten High," he said, laughing. "In fact, don't mind if I do."

Perry reached under the counter and pulled out a fifth of whiskey. He uncapped it, swallowed a snort, and held it out to us. I knew Owens wouldn't pass up a shot. And I took a little swig to be sociable. I never liked whiskey much. I gave Owens a dime to call Sally Ann, let her know we were coming, and he limped to the pay phone outside.

Shuddering a little from the whiskey burn, I walked between aisles of Campbell's soup and Fels-Naptha soap to the refrigerated cases, where I swung open a glass door and grabbed four quart-bottles of Thunderbird. It's not a fancy dinner wine, but it's got kick, and it's what I like.

I set the bottles on the wooden counter. "Let me have a pack of Lucky Strikes too," I said. I didn't smoke, but I knew Owens would want some. Perry punched buttons on the cash register, and black numbers on small metal placards bounced up in the register window. He hit another button and the cash drawer flew open.

"That'll be $6.25," Perry said. I handed him some bills, he gave me back some silver.

Owens and Sally Ann lived in an orange A-frame tourist cabin just north of the Oceanside pier. A half-dozen or so of the two-room cabins faced the water, another row of them lined up behind, strategically placed so each cabin had a view of the water. The front windows, about the size of twin beds, reflected an orange sun kissing the Pacific.

Low tide pulled the water back from the shore. Camel-faced seagulls squawked and squalled, fighting over popcorn that a kid tossed into the air from a paper bag. Two-foot waves foamed toward the beach. A young couple walked holding hands, sharing a concession soda in a big paper cup. A grinning German shepherd in full lope chased shorebirds that cackled in protest as they took flight.

We parked in a courtyard behind the cabin rows, and the pier lights snapped on as we stepped out.

"I don't think she's here yet," Owens said. "But let's go in and have a drink."

"Fine by me," I said.

He used his keys to get us through the front door of number four. The living room and kitchen were in front. I imagined in the back was a bathroom and bedroom, but the connecting door was closed, so I couldn't see. Knotty-pine walls shone with some kind of shellac. The furniture was shabby but clean. A green davenport. A couple of straight-back chairs. A coffee table with one *Life* magazine and a cut-glass bowl with mixed nuts. A table with four chairs in the kitchen. A gas stove, a refrigerator, a sink, and some cupboards for the dishes and soup pots. All very clean and very spare.

Owens handed me two glasses. At my place we never used glasses. But we were uptown now, I guessed. So I cracked open a bottle of wine and filled two glasses. He put the other bottles in the refrigerator. Owens took a drink. His wide nostrils widened as he gulped. His pale reddish hair caught the light from the setting sun. He flipped on a wooden table radio and Conway Twitty twanged through the cheap speaker.

"You have it good here, man," I said.

"Oh, hell yes. My Sally Ann is the best. She takes care of me," he said.

A few minutes later, Sally Ann trudged through the door, carrying a grocery bag that was almost as big as she. She wasn't much more than three feet tall, with a pleasant oval face and brown, curly hair still in a hairnet. She smelled of hamburger grease.

Owens introduced us. She said hello and I could hear the Southern belle in her voice.

"You'll have to excuse me while I change out of these work things," she said. "But it is so nice to meet you. Harold has told me so much about you."

"Not too much, I hope."

"Nothing but good. Nothing but good, my man," Owens said.

Sally Ann slipped into the back room and I could hear her getting changed.

"Would you care for a glass of wine, sugar plum?" Owens asked through the door.

"Is it chilled? It's so been so warm and sticky today, something cool would be refreshing," she said.

"Yeah, it's cold. Straight out of Perry's refrigerator," he said.

She came out wearing lime-green slacks and an orange print blouse of sorts. Her hair was down and she smelled great.

"That would be lovely," she said. Owens got a bottle from the refrigerator and poured her a water-glass full.

"Cheers," she said. She drank. Not a dainty sip, but businesslike swallows. "Now, that does help erase the day, doesn't it?" she said.

"What is it you do, Mr. Max?" she asked, taking another drink.

"Oh, I work construction when I can find it. Hunt and trap in the winter. Fish in the summer. And it's just Max, no need for the 'mister' part. And you?"

"I'm a short-order cook down at the Do Drop Inn. Do you know it? A little place down the highway a mile or two from here."

"Yeah, I may have eaten there," I said. "You mean you been

cookin' all day, and now you're gonna cook some more?"

"Ah, now don't you fret. It'll be no bother. I'm just going to fry some steak and potatoes. Will that do you, Mr. Max?"

"Sounds great," I said.

Sally Ann moved into the kitchen. She scooted a milk crate in front of the stove and stood on it. Owens pulled some steaks from the grocery bag on the table and handed them to her. She threw them into a big frying pan. Some potatoes were already diced and soaking in water in a bowl in the refrigerator. She put some bacon grease in another frying pan and soon poured in the home fries. In no time, dinner was started.

"I hope you menfolk don't mind, but I've invited a lady friend from next door to join us for dinner," she said. She must have called from the café, because I didn't see her use the phone.

Owens didn't seem surprised. "Fine by us," he said.

In a few minutes, knuckles rapped on the front door. Owens yelled, "Come on in, Helena."

Helena was barstool thin, with stiff straw-colored hair that no perm could curl. She waved a Pall Mall between two fingers and carried a tumbler full of iced amber liquid in the same hand.

"Well, hello, y'all," she said, much too chipper.

I was on the couch, and she practically sprinted to the empty spot beside me. She plopped down but didn't make much of an impression in the davenport cushion. "Hello, I'm Helena," she offered her hand.

I shook it. "Max," I said. "Pleased to meet you."

She tried a schoolgirl smile, but wrinkles and a couple of missing teeth wouldn't let her pull it off.

The dinner was eaten, four greasy plates filled the sink. All four bottles of wine were gone. Helena's tumbler was almost empty. Whiskey half closed her lids, and she slurred when she purred.

"I'd sure like to sit in your lap," she said. "You have a mighty inviting lap. I think the curve of my backside would fit nicely in your lap," she cooed, whiskey fumes escaping with each word.

The broom standing in the corner of Sally Ann's kitchen had more curves than Helena. And maybe I wasn't married, but I had a girlfriend that I'd been with for eleven years. And she was true to me. And I was true to her. I sure as hell didn't want to mess that up for the likes of Helena.

"Hey, Owens, man. I gotta be getting home. You gonna drive me?" I asked him. But he didn't have to say anything. I knew he wasn't going anywhere. His chin dropped to his freckled chest. His mouth was slack. His eyes practically crossed.

"Hell, I can't drive," he said. "Just stay with Helena. She's got a good bed next door, and she'll have you, won't you, Helena?"

"Why, sure, you can stay with me," Helena said. "I'd love to have you."

"Go ahead, Mr. Max. Keep Helena company," Sally Ann said.

Helena, smiling up at me with rapacious teeth, ran her hand up and down my leg. "Yeah, stay with me," she said, making circles on my leg with her fingernails, her voice full of syrup.

"Come on, Sally Ann, let's hit the rack, let these two lovebirds have at it," he said. And I knew I had been set up. Owens had engineered this whole thing, getting me here probably as a favor to Sally Ann. Never trust a man who loves a woman. A man will do anything, I mean anything, for a woman he loves. And so here I was, trying to keep an arm's length from this poor creature. I don't consider myself a mean-spirited man. I didn't want to hurt Helena's feelings. But I didn't want to sleep with her either.

"Listen, Helena, I'm bushed. I think I'll just crash on this couch," I said.

"Ohhh myyyy, that has possibilities too. I can fit. I don't take much room," she said.

"No, Helena, you don't get it, I just…"

"Oh, I get it. You're bushed. But I got bush," she said with a leer. Jesus. "Helena, will you please let me sleep?"

"Of course, Max," she said. And she stood. I thought she was going to go. But she didn't. She walked over to the radio, turned it up some, and started doing a striptease, slowly unbuttoning her blouse as Patsy Cline sang, "I go out walkin' after midnight…"

She wasn't wearing a bra. She didn't need one. She jutted two tits no bigger than fried eggs toward my face.

And I went walking. After midnight. It was twenty-eight miles down Highway 76, but I made it home shortly after daybreak. I drank a beer. Took off my shoes. Drank another beer, and went to sleep.

Goddamn Owens. He'd get his. I'd sell him another snake.

SEEING-EYE DOG

DiWayne punches one pillow, covers his head with the other, trying to block sound. No dice. Damn barking dog. Sound infiltrates cotton pillowcases and down feathers to sink spikes into his ears.

From outside his window, the pit bull's bark screeches, high-pitched and shrill, like Mike Tyson vowing to eat babies. Bark. Bark. Bark. It's been at it for two days, ever since arriving. What the hell is it barking at? Barking at strangers would be normal. Barking at a passing dog would be understandable. It would eventually end. But there's nothing out there, and this goes on and on and on. DiWayne opens his eyes, scanning the night, bringing the familiar into focus. The alarm clock's red numbers read 3:36 a.m., less than an hour and a half before he laces on running shoes for roadwork. His stomach grinds and churns, the chile verde eaten for dinner reheating in his gut as heartburn. He flips over to his right side, facing his wife. Her slack face, partially veiled by a tangle of black hair, scrunches like a bloodhound's against her pillow, her lips flapping softly with each exhale. How can she sleep through this?

A night breeze eddies through the open window. Closing the window might muffle some of the sound, but it's at least eighty degrees in the bedroom, and without a breeze, man, the room would bake. DiWayne sleeps naked with just a sheet, and even then his body is greasy and damp with sweat. And, too, DiWayne struggles with claustrophobia. Not enough to trigger an escape in terror from an elevator, but enough to tighten breathing once the doors slide shut. His fight promoter is on the twentieth floor of a Los Angeles office building. When DiWayne visits, he climbs the stairs. Good for the legs, he rationalizes. The real reason—twenty floors makes for too much heart-banging in the casket of an elevator.

DiWayne breathes deep yoga breaths, trying to calm himself. He shuts his eyes to conjure images of someplace pleasant. Go to your happy place, they told him in anger management classes. A while back he did three months for assault in a south-county road camp over a road-rage incident. Some asshole on a Harley cut him off, flipping the bird as he did so. DiWayne caught up to him and returned the gesture. Harley wanted him to pull over. DiWayne obliged. Even though the motorcycle puke threw the first punch, DiWayne did time because he was a boxer. Was he just supposed to stand there, hands down, and let the guy sock him up? As part of his sentence, the judge ordered DiWayne to anger management classes, where they taught relaxation techniques. He tries. DiWayne imagines a Tahitian grass hut, waves foaming against white sand, wind whispering through palm trees, a rock-a-bye hammock, a sloe-eyed Native girl handing him a rum-mango drink in a coconut shell. He listens for the waves, the roll and rush of water lapping onto shore. But there is only BARK. BARK, BARK. Mad, maniacal barking—almost a whistling shriek—from a hellhound possessed.

"Shit," DiWayne utters under his breath, trying not to wake his wife. He throws back the sheet and climbs out of bed, padding barefoot on the wood floor to the window, lowering it slowly, willing it to close quietly. It squeaks, though. It needs oiling. He looks over at his sleeping wife, who doesn't stir. DiWayne doesn't want to deal with her *and* the barking dog. He returns to bed, tugging the sheet over his shoulder, nestling his head into the pillow. Bark. Bark. Bark. Still loud, maybe down one number on the volume control, but still loud. The dog's pitch is croaking, its throat barked dry, but it won't stop, not even for a drink of water. Christ.

DiWayne has a fight Saturday night, the night after next. He's matched against Jose "Mambo" Morales, a tough Tijuana kid, tireless and whipcord fast. At thirty-five DiWayne probably should retire. He isn't sure why he's still fighting, but he is. His daddy was a prizefighter; his uncle too. It's in his blood.

He likes the cheering crowd as he bounces on thin-soled boxing shoes down the walkway toward the ring. He likes the exposed flesh of ring-card girls in thong bikinis radiating sex in the glare of TV lights. He likes climbing through the ropes and feeling he controls his destiny once the bell rings. He likes setting opponents up, then, when it's right, throwing the uppercut they don't see coming. The thump of leather on an unsuspecting jaw that puts out the lights.

He's most alive in the ring. His senses sharpen; his vision accelerates to slow everything down. He calls it his fighter-pilot mode, everything happening in slow motion so he can slip and parry and throw his counters. He's on a winning streak, twelve straight, seven by knockout. He knows it can't last forever, but he doesn't want it to end. Not yet. He bites the inside of his cheek, worried the streak might fizzle over lack of sleep. Thoughts of defeat aren't allowed. Defeat feeds on negativity and doubt. Stay positive. Tough to stay positive, though, when in torment.

Bark. Bark. Bark. Heat reddens DiWayne's face. With the window closed, heat thickens like gravy. He turns onto his back, a position he can't sleep in, but maybe one he can relax in, sucking in air and squeezing it to the very bottom of his lungs, tensing every muscle in every limb, then letting go. He does it again, urging relaxation to settle him down enough for slumber. Wait, the dog has stopped. Crickets chirp. A truck whines down the road. A distant stereo thumps some hip-hop shit, probably the neighbor tweakers revving up over a fresh line. Regular night sounds resume. DiWayne's teeth unclench. Maybe the dog got tired. Maybe it will sleep. Maybe... But no, there it goes, a siren of insanity. The dog is psycho. And butt ugly. Its coat so milky white, pink skin shows through. Its head is wider than body proportions should allow. Thickly muscled, the dog hulks like a juiced-up weight lifter, too ripped for a normal gait. When it barks, its flint eyes roll back into its wedge of a head, revealing a bottom rim of bloodshot white.

The dog never enjoys a playful, puppy moment. It never smiles. It snarls at the end of a fifteen-foot tow chain bolted around the base of an apricot tree, jumping, fighting, choking against the chain at least a hundred fifty times a day. It's broken several teeth trying to bite through the chain. In frustration it bites its own tail, leaving bloody divots that cleave to the bone. Quite simply, the dog is berserk.

It's too hot, the bedroom sweltering and airless with the window shut. DiWayne can't breathe. He throws back the sheet to slide out of bed and eases the window open. It squeaks again. He stands a moment, nose pressed against the dusty screen, inhaling what little there is of a cool breeze. The dog barks, barks, barks. He can see the apricot tree from his bedroom window. He can see the dog through the bushes, standing at the end of its chain, barking. The dog faces DiWayne's bedroom, like he's barking at DiWayne. A half-honeydew moon glowers in the sky. The dog, ghostly in the moonshadows, strains against the chain, steel-trap jaw opening and closing with each bark. What in god's name is with this dog?

"Shut the hell up!" DiWayne yells at Paco. Its name is Paco.

"What the...? Jesus, what's the matter?" shouts his wife, now bolt upright and wide-eyed.

"It's that damn dog. It won't stop barking. I can't sleep."

"Come on back to bed," she says through a yawn. Her head thuds back into her pillow. "I thought the Muslims were attacking."

The dog ignores DiWayne's shouts, and barks and barks and barks.

As DiWayne shuffles to bed, he raps his toes against the metal bed frame. "Sonofabitch!"

"Now what?" Lisa says.

"I think I busted my toe on this stupid bed," Diwanye says, now limping.

"My poor baby's got an owie on his toe," Lisa says, oozing sarcasm.

"If I broke my toe, I can't fight. If I can't fight, there goes the San Francisco trip you wanted. So be a little more sympathetic, won't you?"

Putting things in materialistic terms usually melts Lisa's ice.

"The San Francisco trip was an empty promise just so you could get sex. You're always making promises you don't keep. Why should this be any different?"

Bark. Bark. Bark.

"What are you talking about? I keep my promises. Hell, I even joined the Promise Keepers."

"Lot of good that did. I'm still waiting for that Cadillac Escalade you promised."

"Jesus, Lisa, that was four years ago. And I was drunk."

"A promise is a promise."

"I told you, we don't need a Cadillac Escalade. Hell, we can't even afford gas for an Escalade. Besides I bought you that Denali out front with the fancy rims and the DVD player. What more do you want?"

"I want the Escalade you promised. Now stop arguing and let me sleep."

Lisa hugs her pillow and turns her back on DiWayne. A roll of fat climbs up the back of her neck. More fat bulges like bat wings where her lat muscles should be. She'd promised to lose sixty pounds. She never kept that promise, something DiWayne knows better than to mention. At dinner she ate four tortillas with her chile verde. DiWayne ate half a tortilla and a single cup of chile verde and a single cup of boiled beans. He measured out ever-so-small, ever-so-sad servings on his plate. But he has to be careful about his weight. He is in The Zone, balancing carbohydrates, fats, and protein, the requirements of his boxing regimen. He weighs in tomorrow. Or should he say today? Running an hour and a half at five each morning. Sparring, hitting the heavy bag in the gym two or more hours each night, while Lisa spends her nights sucking Marlboros and dumping money into video poker machines at the casino. Some nights she is just getting home when DiWayne is getting up to run.

DiWayne stretches out next to her. He lifts the hem of her nightgown and cups her left buttock. He feels the edge of her panties follow the curve of her ass cheek. He tries to work his hand closer to the heart of the matter.

"Not a chance, cowboy," Lisa says, knocking his hand away from her.

"Maybe I could sleep if we…"

"Is that what I am for you, a sleeping pill?"

"Come on, Lisa, I'm just…"

"No way, Jose."

DiWayne doesn't buy into the old saw about sex stealing a boxer's legs. Sex might take his mind off that dog and allow him to sleep.

"Just a quickie?" DiWayne says.

"Ain't no such thing as a quickie with you. You'll hump me like you're jumping rope at the gym, on and on...I swear I'm just an exercise machine to you."

Bark. Bark. Bark.

"Now that stupid dog is bugging me. Isn't there something you can do?" Lisa says.

"I could shoot the damn thing."

In the darkness, DiWayne can tell Lisa is thinking.

"You can't shoot the dog. He's your cousin's. You're supposed to be feeding it, not killing it."

Paco belongs to Theresa, DiWayne's first cousin. DiWayne's Uncle Tomcat, Theresa's father, died last month of congestive heart failure. Theresa took the death of her father hard. Lisa is right; DiWayne can't shoot the dog. The death of her dog might undo Theresa in her vulnerable state. She left the dog in DiWayne's care while she arranged to move back to the rez from Long Beach, back into her father's house, the house next to DiWayne's. How could DiWayne tell Theresa he'd shot her dog? No, he couldn't.

"There's some sleeping pills in the drawer next to the sink. Why not wrap one in some meat and feed it to the dog? Maybe it will knock the damn thing out," Lisa says, her back still toward DiWayne.

"Why not? I'll try anything."

DiWayne slips on a robe and switches on the bathroom light to find the plastic bottle in the drawer. Several red capsules rattle inside. Seconal. That ought to send the beast to dreamland. He shakes out two gel caps, carries them to the kitchen, and wraps them in uncooked bacon. He steps out into the night through the back door. The moon illuminates his way along the path to his uncle's yard, where Paco, deranged and slobbering, rears on his two hind legs against the chain. Let's hope that chain holds. How to give him the bacon? From a safe distance, he tosses the little bacon package. It rolls to a stop in front of Paco. DiWayne can see it in the dirt, along with the kibble he hasn't eaten. The bacon wrap is well within reach. Any other dog would eat it. Not Paco. Paco barks and barks and barks, slamming against the chain, lunging, biting the air. DiWayne steps back and squishes an overripe apricot under his bare foot.

"Crap. Eat the danged bacon, Paco," DiWayne says.

Paco, growling, snarling, barking, knife-sharp canines bared and snapping, eyes screaming violence, won't eat the bacon.

If DiWayne goes inside, maybe Paco will eat the bacon. DiWayne backs away and heads toward the house. Paco doesn't let up. DiWayne wipes apricot from his foot on the doormat. A new kind of toe jam, he thinks. He goes to the bathroom and rinses off his foot in the tub. Lisa yells from the bedroom.

"Well?"

"Damn dog won't eat it."

"What?"

DiWayne goes to the bedroom. Lisa sits propped against her pillows, playing a poker game on her smartphone.

"He blew it off. He just let it sit there."

"Do you get the feeling that dog hates you?"

"Hell yeah. I can't get near him."

"How do you feed him?"

"I throw a bunch of kibble at him. I do spray him with the hose when I fill his water bowl, just to raise hell. That pisses him off."

"Maybe that's why he can't stand you."

"He hated me the second he saw me. Good thing Theresa had him on a leash when she took him out of her car. He lunged at me right then. I can't understand it. I've never done nothing to him. Dogs like me, just not this one. It's creepy."

Bark. Bark. Bark.

"I can't sleep now with that going on," Lisa says. "Close the window; maybe that will help."

"Tried it already. It's too hot with it closed."

"I told you to get air conditioning. But noooo. You're so damn cheap, DiWayne."

DiWayne goes into the bathroom, tears off a couple of squares of toilet paper, wads them up, and sticks them in his ears. He returns to bed.

"I don't have much boxing left in me. I'm trying to invest, trying to get us a retirement. I can't invest if you spend all the money before…"

"So that means we get no life. We suffer because you want to save?"

"Can't you just try to be happy? I gotta sleep. First time I ever wished I was deaf."

"Don't say that. Don't say stuff like that. When you say bad things, you invite bad things to happen. You know better."

"Are you sure we can't, you know…"

"Not 'no' but 'hell no'. With that going on? Dream on."

DiWayne shoves his head into the pillow. The toilet paper in his ears does no good. Bad ideas about things he could do to the dog creep in. He wards them off. Theresa and DiWayne grew up together. They were close when they were kids. She was the first girl he ever saw naked. They'd played strip poker in an abandoned house when they were ten. DiWayne cheated to win. Dust motes circled in the sunlight slanting through a broken window. A band of light fell across her skin. DiWayne thrilled at her glow, a strange and mysterious stirring. He reached for her.

"No," Theresa said. "It's not right."

"I don't care," DiWayne said. And he touched her privates.

Theresa shrieked and jumped away. She picked up her clothes and tried to hide behind them. She cried and dirt smudged her right cheek.

"Stop it, DiWayne. You stop it right now, before something bad happens."

DiWayne couldn't contain himself. He backed Theresa into a corner, remnants of daffodil wallpaper peeling from the wall.

"No, DiWayne, no," she said, hysteria growing.

"I'm not going to hurt you, Theresa. I just wanna see."

"I'll tell on you. I swear. I'll tell your dad. I'll tell mine."

"Go ahead and tell."

But DiWayne stopped. Sure, his dad would take a belt to him. But he could stand the welts. But he liked his Uncle Tomcat. He didn't want to get him mad.

"I swear, I wasn't gonna hurt you," DiWayne said.

"Just let me out of here," she said.

It had never been the same between DiWayne and Theresa since then. She wears distance like a shield. Not like when they swam in the river, or sat together at the Fallbrook picture show watching cowboy movies, or climbed the big fig tree behind their aunt's house and sucked the juices out of Mission figs. Back then, Theresa had been more best friend than cousin. But since the strip poker, Theresa won't be alone with him. Over the years, they have continued to be polite. And they do favors for each other. Taking care of the dog, for instance. But Theresa looks at him funny. Mistrust tinges her eyes when they speak. She avoids his gaze if he tries to make eye contact. She never even sends him a card at Christmas. DiWayne wonders how it is going to be living next to her. He'll have to bring the incident up. He'll have to apologize, again, make her understand. They were just kids and it was a stupid, stupid thing he did. She has to forgive. He was wrong. He knows that. It has never happened again—it never will. He'll convince her. He wants things right between them.

Bark. Bark. Bark. Maybe he can make it right with Theresa. Theresa, maybe. But the damn dog?

"Don't you have Theresa's phone number? Call her. Let her hear her dog," Lisa says.

"It's four in the morning. I don't want to call her."

"Why the hell not? What are we going to do? We can't live like this. This is the second night of no sleep."

"Just wait a minute. Maybe it will eat the bacon."

"It would have eaten it by now. He's not eating that bacon on purpose."

"What are you talking about?"

"You know what I'm talking about, DiWayne. That dog is crazy with hate for you."

"It's only been here two days. Maybe it just needs time to get used to the place."

"So are we gonna live in a hotel till it does? That barking is getting to me."

"You were sleeping before."

"Yeah, because I took a pill. I can't sleep now. And I don't want any more pills. And you can't take pills. How will you fight if you're half drugged?"

"Let's just try once more. Close your eyes. Relax. Think happy thoughts. Maybe sleep will come."

But it doesn't. And the dog doesn't stop. Anger ascends from the gut to the head, gushes like blood from a wound, until it consumes reason. DiWayne pants to control his temper. None of the techniques the bald-headed cream puff in the sweater vest made him practice in anger management class work. DiWayne is trapped. Anger and claustrophobia choke him.

Five minutes, ten minutes, fifteen minutes he tries to sleep, but the barking climbs inside him and pokes him with a sharp stick. DiWayne quivers in white heat.

"Fuck," he says, sitting up. He finds his robe on the back of her vanity chair and puts it on again. This time, he runs his foot under the bed until he touches his slippers. He shoves his feet into them. He keeps a loaded semiauto 9 mm Beretta between the mattress and bedspring. He lifts the mattress and grabs the gun by its checkered grip. He pulls the slide back to chamber a cartridge and clicks it closed with finality.

"You're not going to," Lisa says.

"Watch me."

He drops the pistol into his robe pocket and goes back outside. The half moon shines in the night sky, a pearl on jeweler's velvet. DiWayne follows the dirt path through the night-blooming jasmine toward his uncle's. The air is sweet with jasmine scent. His uncle helped to plant the jasmine. He sees his uncle, on his deathbed, a gawky, pinfeathered bird, all beak and hopeless eyes after heart failure stole his strength.

When DiWayne was about five, he'd been playing barefoot in the dirt road across from his grandmother's house. He knelt in the powdery Pala dust and dragged a block of two-by-four to smooth out a road for his Tonka truck. It was a red dump truck with a yellow bed. A silver lever lifted the bed to dump the dirt. It was a birthday gift from his uncle. DiWayne scooped dirt with a tomato-soup can into the bed, then pushed the truck along the dirt road, dumping the dirt into a pile. DiWayne was making a hill, like he'd seen real trucks do. But DiWayne's road ran dangerously close to a mound of red ants. As DiWayne made truck noises with his lips, a red ant sunk its jibs into DiWayne's toe. "Yeow!" DiWayne yowled and ran back to his grandmother's crying.

His Uncle Tomcat was changing the oil in his blue Chevy longbed in the front yard.

"What the hell's the matter, boy?" asked Uncle Tomcat from under the hood.

"An ant bit me," DiWayne said.

"Ouch. That hurts," Uncle Tomcat said.

DiWayne stood there, nodding his head and sniffling, his toe burning.

"We'll fix those damn ants," he said.

He went into DiWayne's grandmother's—Tomcat's mother's—house and came out with a double-barreled shotgun.

"Show me those ants, boy."

DiWayne led him to the anthill where his red dump truck waited, half a load of dirt in the bed. A mess of red ants, jerking in untidy rows, entered and exited the mound. Uncle Tomcat stood to his full height in blue jeans and grease-stained T-shirt and aimed the shotgun at the anthill.

"Better get behind me, boy," Uncle Tomcat said.

BOOM! Uncle Tomcat let both barrels loose. The lead shot tore up the ground like a bomb, blowing ants to kingdom come.

"How do you like that, boy?" Uncle Tomcat said, smiling. "Feel any better?"

And he did. Gratitude lifted the corners of DiWayne's mouth.

"Nothing like a little revenge," Uncle Tomcat said.

Now he's about to shoot the dog of Uncle Tomcat's daughter. And Theresa loves the damn dog. She'd showed DiWayne the new collar she'd beaded for him. Theresa is a storyteller and has a new CD coming out. The beaded collar is to dress up the dog for the CD cover. With each step, DiWayne weighs the rights and the wrongs of his actions. Although no astrology nut, he is a Libra who needed to balance fairness. But there is no way to measure Theresa's love for the dog against his dislike. Doesn't he have some right to some sleep? Do those rights outweigh Theresa's love of the dog? Or is his anger skewing his judgment? Maybe he is too pissed to be rational. Maybe he should wait for light of day.

Bark. Bark. Bark. No, dammit. No waiting.

How will he tell Theresa? Will he tell Theresa? He sees himself concocting a story about thieves coming in the night to take her dog. But no thief could get close enough to take it. It would shred any stranger. Maybe the dog got loose somehow? But DiWayne had given Theresa a nut and a bolt to secure the dog, and she'd tightened the nut herself. It wouldn't loosen without help. Somebody else shot the dog? But who? There was no logic to it. And Theresa looks so sad these days. Looks so orphaned. Her father had raised her without a mother. Her mother had had no maternal instincts and had left Pala *and* her daughter to turn tricks in San Diego, bedding down sailors to feed her drug habit. Her mother died when Theresa was too young to remember much. Killing her dog would rip her heart out. This couldn't happen at a worse time. DiWayne and Paco were all the family she had left.

DiWayne's thin robe lists to the right with the weight of the pistol in the pocket. He slows, then stops in indecision at the gate in the low chain-link fence. Stars blink messages. By Indian way, each star is the soul of an ancestor, but what are they telling him? An owl hoots from a nearby eucalyptus tree. Good sign, or bad? DiWayne doesn't know. He should have paid more attention when his grandfather explained those kinds of things.

Bark. Bark. Bark. DiWayne continues. The dog knows DiWayne is coming. It's like he knows why, too. Paco leaps skyward, twisting in midair trying to shake off the chain, like a marlin trying to shake the hook. He's frothing at the mouth. Maybe he's got rabies? But DiWayne knows Theresa would vaccinate him. Wouldn't surprise him if she did it herself, bought a syringe at the pet store and inoculated him. Theresa was good with animals that way.

Paco lands on all fours and stands, snarling at DiWayne. Can this dog see into the future? Does he know what DiWayne's gonna do? Has he always known? Some people could see into the future. Why not dogs? DiWayne sees Paco would kill if he could. Diwayne can smell Paco's hate. It smells the way bile tastes. Paco would spring for the throat and clamp on, rip with vicious shakes of the head until DiWayne's jugular was torn and Paco's jaws were soaked in blood. Paco would kill DiWayne in a heartbeat. In the law of nature, in the kill-or-be-killed world, is it wrong for DiWayne to kill Paco first?

DiWayne stands about five feet from Paco. He takes the pistol, its grip nestled into his hand. Paco rears and rears, choking himself against the chain, his tendons and muscles bulging in fury. DiWayne raises the gun and aims, lining up the pistol sights, dimly lit by moonlight, on Paco's huge head. Twenty years ago, there would have been no hesitation. The dog would have been dead. It was the reservation rule. Dogs had to fit into human life or die. Chase a cow, get shot. Bite a kid, get shot. Bark endlessly, get shot. But the reservation has changed, civilization softening the rules. Now DiWayne suffers doubts. By old Indian ways, the dog would be dead. Hell, in the old days, that dog might have been supper. But the new, gentler Indian takes anger management classes and seeks nonviolent solutions. But DiWayne has a fight Saturday night, a fight he must win. He can't let a dog, a stupid no-account dog, ruin his fight career, his whole future. He could be a super-middleweight champ. He still has time. He has the punch. He has the fire. He will step into the ring with a night's sleep. DiWayne nods goodbye and squeezes the trigger. BOOM! The pistol jumps. Paco drops. Paco's obsidian eye stares at eternity. Blessed quiet. Maybe he's done Paco a favor. No more fighting the chains of life. No more hate. No more insanity. No more...He will think of something to tell Theresa. For now, there is dead silence, except for the owl voicing opinions—hopefully absolutions—from a nearby eucalyptus tree.

UNHOLY WINE

Thick magnolia leaves, nudged by a Pacific breeze, worried the bedroom windowpanes. Leaves scraping against glass, an antique clock ticking off time, a cat mewling in another room—other than that, fatal silence prevailed. On the nightstand, next to the single bed, lay a leather-bound *Lives of the Saints* open to the chapter on St. Augustine. On the bed lay the dead priest.

The adobe room smelled of incense, lemon-oil furniture polish, and the sheared-copper odor of blood. Not all blood smells bad. Whenever we butchered a pig at my place, Angelita, a neighbor, who ten thousand cigarettes ago was a roller derby queen, placed a dishpan beneath the hanging carcass to catch the blood streaming from its slit throat. While my cousin and I skinned for chicharrónes, she'd disappear into her Airstream trailer to fry the blood into a kind of clabbered pudding with onions and cilantro. In a little while, she brought out the pan of blood pudding with some flour tortillas and we ate fried-blood burritos with yellow chilies in the shade of a gnarled pepper tree.

That blood was okay. Good, in fact. Most blood, though—not so good. As a former deputy sheriff, my days were awash in it. I responded to countless bloody car wrecks, knifings, shootings, and beatings. I know the smell of blood too well.

The priest's lifeblood—corpuscles of childhood memories mingled with a thousand disappointments and much-too-brief joys—puddled in the grout of the rectory's terra-cotta tile. Blood also seeped into the pillow, into the sheets, into the mattress, and splattered Pollock-style onto white plaster walls.

The dead priest faced the wall, with the top sheet tucked under his chin, his balding head nestled in the red-drenched pillow. Blood and brain tissue erupted from just above his ear. On the floor, a heavy, chrome-headed framer's hammer reflected morning sunlight. Brain tissue and bits of sandy-brown hair clung to the checkered hammerhead.

On this June morning, Father Juliano, the Mission San Felipe priest, wouldn't be buttoning up the black cassock hanging over his desk chair. No, this morning, his liturgical prayers would go unsaid.

"Did you know him, Roddy?" Deputy Hinton asked.

"Yeah, I knew him," I said. "I'm not a regular churchgoer, so I didn't know him well. But I knew him. He seemed like a decent guy, a good priest."

"Well, somebody didn't like him," Hinton said.

"Evidently," I said.

*E*arlier that morning, the cell phone ringer interrupted my stretching exercises. I should have turned the damn thing off.

"Roddy? This is Willie," said Willie Portillo, a tribal cop I've known all my life.

"Yeah?" I said.

"Looks like someone killed Father Juliano last night."

"No way. You're kidding."

"Nope. He's in his bed with a bashed-in skull."

"Whoa. Who'd want to kill a priest, for Christ's sake?"

"You wanna chance to help find out?"

I had a ten-day Idaho fishing trip planned for next week. A full-on murder investigation would likely mean delay. Half my gear was packed, and I was eager to jump into the Bronco and head for a favorite high-country lake where the trout fought hard, then fried up crisp in a campfire skillet.

"I don't know, Willie, I got something else cookin'," I said.

"Who are you bullshitting! You know you're gonna work this. It's in your blood, man. Besides, Malcolm's already asked for you."

"Is he even around?"

"Naw, he's in Sacramento, but we called him as soon as we found out."

"He wants me in?"

"He wants you in."

I took an early retirement four years ago as a San Diego County Sheriff's Department investigator after a gangbanger's bullet plowed through my right hip and left me with a limp. But the San Felipe tribe still hires me now and then to work on tricky cases. And to be truthful, I like investigating. For one thing, I believe in justice. There's too little of it in the whirlpool of greed and inhumanity we live in. For another thing, investigating invigorates me, makes me feel more alive. I'm a bird dog with a nose full of quail when I'm working a case.

I backed out of the priest's bedroom and stepped into the shadowy hall, where Willie Portillo, a burly guy with a gentle voice, consoled Mrs. Nuskat, the graying housekeeper, who sniffled into a handkerchief. She sat with shoulders hunched in a wooden chair, a shaft of sunlight illuminating her collapsed face.

"We're gonna find who did this thing, Rainy," he said. He talked low and soft. Rainy Nuskat was some kind of cousin to Willie.

"He was a good priest, Willie. You guys were supposed to keep him safe. You're security, aren't you?" Her voice, echoing in the empty hall, croaked through her tears. I returned to the bedroom.

A green-backed fly, stuck in the drying blood, buzzed in frantic circles on the floor.

"Looks like the perp came through the bedroom door," said Hinton, a freckled, ginger-topped San Diego sheriff's deputy I'd known for more than ten years. His khaki shirt, with the deputy sheriff's patch on the sleeve, strained to cover his Kevlar vest and pitchers-of-draft belly.

Careful not to touch anything, I studied the open window above the bed. The window's screen hadn't been messed with. Undisturbed dust and dried green paint chips filmed the sill.

"Nobody's climbed through this window recently," I said.

"It doesn't look like he struggled much. His bedsheets and blanket aren't even mussed," Hinton said.

"Ever see a steer get sledgehammered in the head for butchering?" I said. "They drop to the ground, twitch a little, and die. Not much thrashing."

The hammer had punched through the priest's skull the way it might bust a hole in sheetrock. But there was so much cranial damage the assailant might have swung more than once.

"Shit," he said, shaking his head, running freckled fingers through his close-cropped hair. His stomach grumbled. It always grumbled. He had the noisiest innards of anyone I knew. He stifled a burp with his fist. "I radioed the crime lab. They should be here in a few."

"We need to get Mrs. Nuskat out before they get here. This place will be crawling," I said.

Back when I was still a deputy sheriff, Hinton and I partnered in Fallbrook for a couple of years. We had equal rank back then. Those were good days for us—busting drunks for smash-and-grabs at the Friendly Village Liquor Store, chasing avocado thieves down pitch-black grove roads, rolling up to sprawling red-tile-roofed houses where pilots' wives crashed and burned on too many tranquilizers and vodka gimlets, miserable in their satin nightgowns and press-on nails, teacup poodles licking their rouged cheeks slackened against parquet floors.

Hinton and I had survived our share of mayhem. After I'd left the force, I often worked with him in my role as tribal consultant/ investigator. He didn't mind when the tribe called me in on cases. We worked good together.

San Felipe, a reservation of about twenty thousand acres and a thousand or so Luiseño members, pays the county sheriff's department $100,000 a year for extra law enforcement. There's a deputy assigned to the reservation, and that deputy is often Hinton.

Hinton said, "Yeah, we better clear everyone out."

Hinton and I left the bedroom and walked through the hall to where Mrs. Nuskat continued to sniffle.

A century-old wood-framed black-and-white photograph of the mission campanile hung above the chair Mrs. Nuskat sat in. In the photo, a Luiseño man, woman, and child stood frozen in time in front of the bell tower. Mrs. Nuskat resembled the woman in the photograph. Both were dark, both wore aprons, and both aprons puffed out in a way that spelled too many tortillas and beans.

Hinton touched her shoulder to get her attention. "Mrs. Nuskat, the forensics team will be here soon. We have to clear out. Is there anyone else in the building?" Hinton asked.

Mrs. Nuskat wiped her eyes with a crumpled blue bandana. But she didn't wipe her nose, and a trickle of clear mucus dripped from her nostril toward her upper lip. She felt it and blew her nose into the bandana.

"Brother Paul lives in a room along the hall," she said, an arthritic finger pointing the way. "But I don't think he's in there."

"No?" Hinton asked.

"He usually works in the vineyard till lunch," she said.

"What time did you get here this morning, Mrs. Nuskat?" I asked.

"The usual time, eight o'clock. When I get here, Father Juliano's usually just finished saying Mass. He says Mass every morning at seven, even when no one comes. When I get here, he's usually sitting in the study, reading the morning newspaper. But he wasn't this morning. I figured he must be talking to someone after Mass. So I started breakfast. But eight thirty came and his eggs and linguica—he liked linguica—were getting cold. I went to find him. I knocked on his door. He didn't answer."

"His door was closed?" I asked.

"Uh-huh, that's why I knocked."

"Was his door locked?"

"No, he never locked it. I just opened it to peek in. And I saw the blood on the floor and on his pillow. I went to him. I touched his wrist for a pulse. But he felt cold. He felt dead."

"He never locked the door?"

"No, no. He said locked doors were for people with something to hide," she said. And she started crying again. "Why would anyone want to hurt him? He was a holy man."

Willie eased her to her feet and escorted her out the front door, while Hinton and I headed for Brother Paul's room, about twenty-five feet down the long hall from Father Juliano's. We knocked. No answer. He wasn't there, just like Mrs. Nuskat predicted, but plenty

and whatever meat they could muster. Maybe he liked the way she made her frybread. I don't know. Anyway, they married and had several children. I still carry the Foo name and some of his blood and his Taoist inclinations. When I was a kid, I bloused the eye of more than one guy who called me chink and gook, even though I wasn't sure what a gook was, but it didn't sound like a compliment. And I'd start swinging. I guess that was the Indian side of me doing the fighting. Soon they stopped calling me names.

I still feel divided that way. I want peace and harmony. I wish no harm to anyone. But the Indian side of me, well, that side isn't opposed to kicking a little ass every now and then if necessity demands it.

I got on the phone and called Chairman Purdy. He's another guy I've known since childhood. It took several minutes to locate him in his Sacramento hotel room.

"Purdy?"

"Yeah."

"This is Foo. There's a new cop, a Captain Willows, who's bitching about me being on the case."

Purdy laughed some, a horsey little snicker. I could imagine his loose jowls flapping. "Gave you a little hassle, did he?"

"Well, yeah."

Purdy laughed again. He was enjoying himself. "Okay, don't get your panties in a wad. I'll make some calls."

I cruised up San Felipe Mission Road, the old eucalyptus trees lording it over the village of mostly older homes. New, bigger homes were being built in adjacent areas. A big yellow dog ran out from Frank Mesa's ramshackle house. It was an old Ridgeback cross, well known for biting tires. Someday that dog's gonna get run over, people tell Frank. But Frank knows better. He just sticks his hands beneath the bib overalls and smiles. "I keep telling that dang dog to knock it off, but he just won't listen," he says. The dog is twelve years old if he's a day, and he's still chasing tires. He's never been scratched by a car.

I kept a steady pace as I passed Frank's yellow house. I watched in my mirrors as the dog peeled off after about fifty feet, his tongue lolling, a grin on his face.

I parked up at the mission school and walked around back, behind the adobe wall where Brother Paul was building his cross of chromed hubcaps. He was there all right, in black pants and a gray sweatshirt with the sleeves cut off, a pear-shaped man in his forties wobbling atop a ladder; nailing an Oldsmobile hubcap to the cross. He had reached the top of his ladder; he'd need a scaffold or a cherry picker or a taller ladder to get any higher.

I walked to the ladder's base and Brother Paul kept working. It had to be a twenty-five-footer, one of the kind used for picking fruit. His feet were planted on the rung second from the top. The ladder shifted as Brother Paul swung his hammer.

I called up at him. "Aren't you worried you'll fall?"

"The thought has crossed my mind, but the cross won't get built if I don't do it."

"Mind taking a break while I ask you a few questions?"

"You're Rodney Foo, and you're investigating Father Juliano's death, I'm guessing?"

"Yep."

"Okay, down in a sec." Brother Paul clambered down, his butt way wider than his shoulders. When his Doc Martens hit the ground, he turned around to face me. His nose and cheeks were flushed, riddled with the tiny red veins of a man who nipped the sacramental wine a little too often. Wiry brows bushed from his forehead. Sweat dappled his shaved dome. Thick wire-rimmed glasses blurred the pale blue of his eyes. His small, fine-boned hands, a jeweler's hands, gripped a chrome-headed framer's hammer.

He pulled off his glasses and rubbed the lenses clean with the bottom of his sweatshirt. School was out for summer, so the adjacent playing fields were silent of screaming kids playing ball. Instead of screeching kids, you could hear songbirds trilling in tree branches.

"What an awful thing to have happen," he said.

"That's for sure. Your room is just down the hall from Father Juliano's. Did you hear anything last night?"

"No, I slept like the dead. Now, why did I put it that way?" He forced a perplexed look on his face and scratched his head. I couldn't tell if he was serious or not. People thought of Brother Paul as sort of looney tunes. Nobody thought he was all there.

He loosened and tightened his grip on the hammer handle, his thin fingers turning white with the pressure.

"So you didn't hear a thing?"

"Nothing."

Now what? Something about him threw me off balance. I didn't know how to proceed. When in doubt, stick to small talk. I looked at his project. The hubcap cross ascended higher than thirty feet.

"Looks like you've been busy. How high do you think she'll get?" I asked, looking up at the cross.

"I'm thinking about fifty feet. It feels right to be working on it again."

"You stopped?"

"Father Juliano ordered me to." His watery eyes distorted behind thick lenses. I couldn't tell what he was looking at.

"Yeah?"

"He said he couldn't have me turning the back of the mission into a junkyard. I couldn't seem to get him to understand that this cross was asked for by God the Father. I was commanded to build it."

"Did he want you to tear it down?"

"He did. But I refused. Taking it down was going too far. God's orders take priority. Sorry as I am that the good padre is dead, it does free me to work on this cross again."

The brother had wasted no time. A fresh load of hubcaps overflowed the bed of the mission's rusty Ford pickup. No doubt once the priest was dead he'd made a run to Pistol Pete's junkyard across the river for a fresh load of hubcaps.

"Who pays for the hubcaps?" I asked him.

He hesitated, his lips curling into a sneer. "I do. Why?"

"Just wondering."

"You think I'm nobody. You think I'm nothing. It's an unchristian thing to say, but heck, fella, I could buy and sell you. Don't you worry about money. I've got mine. I'm not absconding church funds to buy hubcaps."

Maybe he had a rich uncle who'd died and left him piles. Hell, I didn't know.

"How did you find out about Father Juliano's death?"

"Ah, a change in the line of questioning, I see. I was clipping hedges in the patio, not far from his bedroom window, when I heard Mrs. Nuskat scream. I ran to his window and saw horror on her face. At my angle, I couldn't see what was wrong, so I ran to his room and stood in the doorway with Mrs. Nuskat. It was awful. I made the sign of the cross and told her not to move or touch anything."

"You didn't see or hear anything out of the ordinary, then?" I asked.

"I sleep hard," he said. "Like the..."

"Dead. Yeah, I know."

Fuchsia and tangerine lights flashed around a video billboard announcing a casino performance of Jim Gaffigan. It was hard to believe. Jim Gaffigan in San Felipe? It wasn't so long ago even the tumbleweeds didn't come to San Felipe. Too boring. I veered right, toward the multilevel parking garage, and found an empty slot on the third level. I kept to the garage's shade, the June sun heating up the day. At the elevators that led to the entrance, a Vietnamese woman in a red brocade jacket held a spiky-haired youth by the elbow. She spoke to him in Vietnamese. I couldn't tell if she was happy or mad, but she was animated.

The casino's main glass door swooshed open at my arrival. An older gent in a blue blazer and striped tie welcomed me with a nod and bade me good luck. I stepped into the cigarette stink of the cavernous gambling room, my feet sinking into deep carpet. Video slot machines beckoned in odd-angled rows, like a Rite Aid drugstore forcing merchandise front and center, prompting the impulse buy. Modern marketing.

It was Wednesday afternoon, a slow time of the day, yet scores of gamblers slouched in vinyl seats, transfixed before electronic screens of spinning numbers willing red sevens into a line. For every celebratory shout of a big win, hundreds set their jaws against mounting losses. Crazy thing is, even when they do win, they can't wait to dump the money back into the machine. I don't get it.

I made my way through intent gamblers toward the bar. I found a stool and motioned to the bartender, a suave Mexican guy, Ramon, I knew from my occasional casino forays for dinner and live music.

"The usual?" he asked, his hair slicked back with brilliantine. I recognized the smell. It smelled like grammar school.

I nodded and he brought me a tall club soda with three limes. Club sodas were free, but I tipped him a couple of bucks.

"Hey, Ramon, you seen a tall, classy-looking woman in here?

She has brown hair kinda cut like Farrah Fawcett, wears white sunglasses and smokes brown cigarettes?"

"Lotta girls in here, boss."

"She's Italian, extremely beautiful, with a rack you can't take your eyes off."

Ramon smiled.

"You must mean Nicole."

"Yeah."

"Why, you trying to hook up with her?"

"Well, just say I'm interested. Does she show up at a usual time?"

"I've only served her twice, at different times of day. She drinks cosmopolitans made with Stoli. She can put 'em away. But, Fooman, both times I seen her, she was with a dude. You sure she ain't married?"

"Not really. What's the guy look like?"

"Tall, middle-aged, graying at the edges, sporty dresser, a scotch-on-the-rocks drinker."

"They look married to you?"

Ramon looked up at the ceiling and squinted in thought. "Naw, probably not. She was a little too attentive. Fingers on his face, lots of kissing, tits on display, all for effect. I'd say him and her was doing it, though. They had that sex look."

Ramon was a bartender with more people smarts than most psychologists.

"All that just from serving her a drink?"

"Like you say, she's an eyeful. Anyway, I don't think you got scratch enough for her, boss."

"So it was like that, huh?"

"Plain, she likes the bling," he said. "Just her cigarette lighter probably cost half a grand."

"Yeah, she does looks expensive, all right. But maybe she's worth it."

"Maybe, but likely not," he said.

I took a drink of club soda, let the ice clink against my teeth.

"Were they in here last night?" I asked.

"I don't know. I wasn't on last night. You'll have to ask Steve or one of the other night bartenders."

He turned and whistled his way down the bar to serve a three-hundred-pound guy in a canary-yellow linen shirt a Drambuie on the rocks.

It was getting late in the day, but coffee percolated in an aluminum pot atop Mrs. Nuskat's stove inside her old adobe house. She sat on a blue vinyl chair at the kitchen table, puffing a Pall Mall, gray hair falling into her eyes. A low-watt bulb burned in the ceiling light fixture, the glass cover littered with moth carcasses. But her kitchen was clean, the drainboard free of toast crumbs. Mrs. Nuskat poured coffee into a brown mug for me.

"Cream and sugar?" she asked.

I don't drink coffee much, especially so late in the day. I like to sleep at night. But I thought drinking coffee with Mrs. Nuskat might put her at ease. Coffee flavored her life. She had to be close to seventy years old, yet still maintained a coffee-and-cigarettes lifestyle. No doubt doctors at the clinic told her to quit. But she wouldn't. Not now. I figured they'd put her in her grave with a coffee cup and a pack of smokes.

"Please, a little of both," I said.

She handed me a can of PET evaporated milk and a sugar bowl. I poured some milk in and spooned in a little sugar. Mrs. Nuskat took another drag of her cigarette.

"I never smoke in the rectory," she said, trying to assure me, and also somehow proud of her own professional code.

"Father Juliano didn't smoke?"

She snorted, smoke escaping from her nose. "Are you kidding? He hated cigarettes."

"What about Brother Paul?"

"I never seen him smoke, but who knows what goes on in his room. I never go in there. His wine breath in the mornings can wilt flowers. Yuck."

"Did you ever hear him argue with Father Juliano about that cross he's building?"

"I wouldn't call it an argument," she said. She picked up her jadeite coffee cup and slurped. "But they did have words. Brother Paul was ticked about having to stop work on it."

"No shouting, though?"

"Not that I ever heard." A fat dachshund, belly almost dragging the floor, waddled into the kitchen on stubby legs. The dog stopped and sniffed my pant cuffs. He probably smelled Soupbone, my old greyhound, on my pants.

"There you are, Gretchen," Mrs. Nuskat said. She picked the dog up and set it on her lap. "She must have been sleeping in the closet."

Gretchen's shiny eyes bulged in the direction of the bear claws on a platter. Mrs. Nuskat tore off a piece, and Gretchen's sharp little teeth snatched it up.

"Did you oil the door hinges?" I asked her.

"What?"

"Did you oil the hinges on the door to Father Juliano's room?"

"Oh, yeah, I did. About a week ago. With that spray oil. I usually do it every six months or so. If I don't, they screech like a dying cat."

My cell phone rang.

"Excuse me," I said, reaching into my pants pocket to retrieve the phone.

"Yep?" I said.

"We picked up Alex Mendez for questioning a half an hour ago," Hinton said.

"I figured that would happen. Willows pushing the buttons?"

"Yeah. But here's something else: Captain Willows found a bunch of letters in Father Juliano's desk. Most of them were from Father Juliano's father, written in Italian. We had them translated."

"Yeah? Can I see them?" I didn't tell Hinton I had found those letters.

As I talked, Mrs. Nuskat fed the doxie sweet rolls. She chomped happily at the treat, licking Mrs. Nuskat's fingers for every crumb. No wonder the dog was so fat.

"Are you trying to get me fired? Willows told me to cut you off. He doesn't like you, by the way. But there was also a bunch of legal papers. It seems our Father Juliano was a millionaire many times over."

"How so?"

"His father had a huge vineyard and winemaking company. He left it all to Father Juliano."

"Nothing to the sister?"

"Nothing. Well, except for a promise that the estate would pay for her college tuition should she decide to go."

So Nicole wasn't lying.

"I'd like to see those translations."

"No can do."

"Remember when you slid off the road and wrecked the patrol car, and I told the captain it was a hit-and-run?"

"Now, this is a different deal. You can't bring up ancient history and…"

"Come on, Hinton, you owe me."

"Okay, I'll make copies. But if I get fired, you gonna feed my kids?"

"You won't get fired," I said. "Purdy's talking to the county supervisors. He'll get Willows straightened out."

"Okay, then. Meet me at the San Felipe Store just before it closes at six. I can't copy everything, there's too much. But I'll pull what looks important and copy that for you."

"'Bout time you came through."

"Screw you, Foo." It was a favorite Hinton comeback; the rhyme of it sounded like old times.

I returned the phone to my pocket and asked Mrs. Nuskat, "Do you think Brother Paul killed Father Juliano?"

If anybody could sense murderous intent in Brother Paul, I guessed Mrs. Nuskat had the best shot at it. I knew Mrs. Nuskat to be a keen observer, one who didn't let on that she knew what was going on.

She fed Gretchen another half a bear claw. "Lordy, how am I supposed to know?" She leaned back and billowed smoke toward the ceiling. "No, I don't think he did it. Maybe he's a bit goofy, and he drinks too much, but a killer? Naw. I'm thinking not Brother Paul."

"Who do you think did it, then?"

"Not Alex, that's for sure. I think the cops are way off on that one."

"How did you know about him?" I hadn't said anything while I was on the phone to Hinton.

"Rez grapevine. You have your sources, I have mine," she said, sipping coffee.

"And why not Alex?" I asked. "Who knows how far a guy will go when he thinks his son has been molested."

"True. But like you, I've known Alex all his life. He might have beaten Father, but he wouldn't sneak into his room to bash his skull with a hammer. That's too far from who Alex is."

"Has anyone accused Father Juliano of molestation before?"

"No. Nobody. Not nobody," she said. "I don't know who did it, but I doubt molestation had anything to do with it." She slurped again. Her coffee couldn't be hot, but she slurped anyway. She coughed her way to the front door as she showed me out.

"One thing: I saw the hammer, the one used to…The one I saw on Father Juliano's floor. It sure looked like Brother Paul's hammer."

"What made you think that?"

"It looked like the one I seen in the workshop where Brother Paul keeps his tools."

"Well, a lot of hammers look alike."

"Yeah, but Brother Paul had his initials on the handle of his."

"So, Brother Paul, you didn't mention that it was your hammer that killed Father Juliano," I said.

Brother Paul was finishing up for the day, picking up discarded hubcaps.

"I know I didn't. That would surely incriminate me. Best to let you figure that one out, you know, earn your pay."

"Yeah, but in the spirit of cooperation, stuff like that is kind of important to the investigation."

"Not really."

I eyed him questioningly.

"My hammer is right there," he said, pointing to his hammer, along with some other tools in an orange plastic bucket in the pickup bed.

"Mind if I take a look?"

"Go right ahead."

I reached over the truck bed and picked up the hammer. And sure enough, there on the handle, lettered with a wood-burning tool, were the initials BPB.

"These are your initials?"

"Yep. My name is Paul Branciforte. Brother Paul Branciforte."

"Mrs. Nuskat said she recognized your hammer on the floor of Father Juliano's bedroom."

"She might have. You see, I have several hammers all the same. But this one has been in the truck for weeks. I keep the others in the toolshed."

"Let's go see," I said.

The toolshed had formerly been the reservation jail. From the early 1900s to the 1950s, the BIA employed a cadre of Indian cops to enforce order. Any number of infractions—leaving the reservation without a permit, insubordination against BIA officials, fighting or being drunk in public—could land you in this ten-by-twenty-foot concrete hot box, or cold box in winter. Although converted these days to a workshop of sorts, there were still bars set in the windows and a heavy metal door. My grandfather used to tell of miserable drunk times spent in here, hungover, oven-hot with the sun scorching the tin roof, the stench of urine or worse in the piss bucket.

A solid workbench sporting a serious vise took up the back of the room. Saws, hammers, pipe wrenches, hedge trimmers, tools of all sorts were flung haphazardly about, victims of Brother Paul's organizational approach.

On the workbench I spotted a hammer that looked exactly like the murder weapon, including the initials burned into the handle. I spied another in a milk crate atop a pile of crap: an old-fashioned hand drill, a mitre box and saw, a cat's-paw, a small pry bar, other tools. Identical hammer, same initials on the handle.

Waving his arm in front of the mess, he said, "As you can see I'm not a fastidious man, so I frequently misplace stuff. My theory is to buy several of the items most often used so I'll always have them at hand. In my room I probably have five pairs of the same glasses lying around."

"You don't lock this place up?"

"No, I have no clue where the key is. I've never even seen it. And I've been at this mission for ten years or more. Anybody could have come in here to snatch a hammer."

He was right. I couldn't pin the hammer to him. He could have used his own hammer on Father Juliano, but it didn't make sense to me. Brother Paul may be nuts, but he didn't come off as a total idiot.

I walked over to the store to meet Hinton. A couple of rez dogs lolled out front. Hinton's black-and-white, a Ford Explorer, rolled up as I arrived. He didn't even get out of his rig. He just handed me a folder of papers through the open window.

"Remember, you didn't get those from me."

"Yeah, yeah," I said. "So what's up?"

"Things seem to be going nowhere fast. Are you on to anything?"

"No, man, nothing is making sense yet. How did Alex hold up?"

"Cap'n Willows is still holding him, but I don't think there's anything there."

"I didn't think so either. Who else? Brother Paul is a strange cat, but I'm not getting guilty vibes from him either. Alex's son told him that Father Juliano had molested him. Maybe Brian did it?"

"I don't know. What do you think?"

"Brian is thirteen. He's a good-sized kid, so it's physically possible. He was an altar boy; he knew the rectory layout. But using a hammer to crush a skull is a tall order for a kid. And Brian is a good kid. I'm thinking he's not our guy."

"Forensics said it was Brother Paul's hammer that was used, but they didn't find any prints, nothing to tie him to it. Somebody used gloves," Hinton said.

"I asked Brother Paul about the hammer. He has several of the same hammers, along with other tools, stored in the old jailhouse. Anybody could have snagged one," I said.

"What about the priest's sister?" Hinton asked.

"Have you seen her?"

"No, not yet."

"You need to. She's gorgeous. Better looking than Claudia Cardinale."

"Claudia Cardinale?"

I shook my head in mock disgust. "Beautiful Italian actress from the sixties. Google her."

"Okay, college boy."

Hinton has always had a thing about my college degree and his lack of one. For most of US history, the Indian has been the uneducated one in the room. Things get a little tricky when the reverse is true.

"So go to college. I'm not stopping you. That way you could learn something besides the difference between imported and domestic beer."

"Smart-ass," he said. We both laughed. It was an old routine.

"I'll probably go see the sister tonight. She's staying at the casino hotel. She drinks cosmopolitans, whatever they are. She's seriously pissed about getting cut from her father's will. She thinks her brother, Father Juliano, talked dirt about her to the father and that's why she got axed. Probably cost her about twenty-five million euros. Did she kill her brother? I don't know. But she had twenty-five million reasons *to* kill him."

*O*nce home, I showered in my wooden shower stall, the one I tiled with a Cahuilla basket design. I adjusted the showerhead to a needle spray, as hot as I could stand it, and scrubbed at the day's grief and grime with a loofah and a bar of glycerin soap. I slipped into a terry-cloth robe and walked out into the living room. Soupbone, my rescue greyhound, slept curled on my couch. I'd long ago quit trying to keep him off the furniture. He felt entitled. And he was mainly a mellow dog, except when in full stride after a rabbit. When on the run, he was a mix of intensity and grace, muscular yet streamlined, perfection of design.

I sat at my dining room table with a cup of hot tea. It wasn't often that I wished for a beer anymore, but I wished for one now. I ate a bean burrito, drank the tea, and unclasped the manila envelope to read Father Juliano's translated letters.

They were simple father-to-son letters. It was clear they loved each other and the father was proud of his son's work. But the letters turned into diatribes against Nicole. I didn't see Father Juliano's letters, so quite possibly they fanned the flames, but the father blamed himself for her excesses. After her mother died in the scuba accident, he had spoiled the girl. He had bought her expensive cars, sent her to expensive private schools, indulged her every whim. When she got kicked out of those schools for drinking and drugging and cheating, he hired tutors to get her through high school. But Nicole had a taste for cocaine, high fashion, gold jewelry, and high-priced art. She ate in the best restaurants, played in the world's finest resorts, drank cocktails, and had sex with the playboys of the Western world. Her father even called her a playgirl.

The father explained he was leaving the winery to Father Juliano and cutting Nicole out. He figured she had already spent her inheritance. Instead of being appreciative, she was getting worse, expecting the world to be laid at her feet. The more her father urged her independence, the worse her manipulations, protestations, and tantrums got.

I put the letters down. My shoulders sank. I had liked Nicole. I had been smitten. I wanted her to be better than she apparently was. If I was honest with myself, I wanted her, I wanted to taste her, feel her olive skin, bury my face in her flesh. But I wanted her to be more than a soft place to masturbate. I wanted to respect her, all of her—body and soul. Damn.

I read more letters. The father liked Father Juliano's idea of starting an AIDS hospice in Africa. The plight of AIDS victims grieved him, and his father gave his permission for Juliano to sell the winery after his death to fund the hospice. His father had a severe heart condition and knew death was imminent. The dying man had embraced a hospice being named for him, a way for his name to live on, since a male grandchild carrying his name seemed unlikely.

Enough reading. Let's get a move on, I thought. I trudged to my bedroom to don night clothes: clean jeans, a fresh white button-down shirt, cowboy boots. I fired up the new Waterpik, brushed tangles from my hair, scraped whiskers off my chin with a fancy four-bladed razor I'd seen in a TV commercial but that was no better than any other razor I'd ever used. I splashed on bay rum aftershave. One last look at myself in the mirror. No, Hollywood wouldn't call anytime soon, but I was presentable.

It was about 8:30 p.m., not late by casino standards, but many gamblers already looked bleary-eyed, probably been at it much of the day, automatons pushing the buttons that made rent money disappear. Behind the bar, a Hawaiian-shirted cover band strummed a weary chorus of "Margaritaville" as Ramon blended margaritas. His starched white shirt had wilted during the long shift. Though weary, he poured the frosty potion from a blender into a margarita glass, filling it to the salted brim with no leftovers. How did he get the exact proportions each time without measuring? Witchcraft?

Ramon saw me and darted his eyes to his left. I followed his glance and saw Nicole perched on a barstool, half a cosmo in front of her, half a cigarette in her right hand, half her breasts exposed in a tight white bustier, a half-lit yes-man by her side, slobbering on himself, trying to put the moves on her. This guy couldn't have been her lawyer/friend; he looked too needy. God, she looked good. Her mahogany hair, coiffed in a Rita Hayworth wave, reached to the middle of her sculpted back. At this angle, I couldn't see much of her face, but she seemed to radiate beauty. The bar was half empty, an open barstool to her right. I went to it.

When I sat, she shot a fast look to see who was next to her, then did a double take.

"Ah, the man of my dreams," she said, turning away from the drooler to face me, her lips inviting kisses the way a neon bar sign welcomes a drunk.

"Say hey, Nicole," I said. Ramon brought me a club soda with lime, rolling his eyes at me like I was a lost cause, and walked off.

"So, my friend, we will extend our conversation, yes?" she said, through a half smile.

"I hoped I might find you here and buy you a drink."

"Of course you may buy me a drink, Mr. Roddy. I'm always in favor of that kind of proposition."

The drooler, noticing he was getting cut out, said, "Hey, Nicole, what gives? I been buying you drinks for a couple of hours."

"You'll have to pardon my rudeness, kind sir, but this is the detective I told you about, and he and I must talk business."

Nicole seemed to know exactly when the truth was better than a lie.

"So that means I'm Mr. Nobody, right?" He squinted, likely

trying to sharpen Nicole's blurred image.

"I'm afraid so, Mr. Freddy, at least for the moment," she said.

He fumbled to his feet and gave her the google-eye weaving in his khakis and wingtips, his head sweating beneath his comb-over. He looked like he wanted to say something, but instead shook his shrunken head and waved goodbye with his bad finger. He departed with the practiced step of someone trying, but not succeeding, to conquer drunkenness.

Nicole sighed. "Well, I guess I didn't make a friend there."

"Nope, don't look for a Christmas card from him," I said.

She drained her cosmo. "Onward, I guess. About that drink?" she said to me.

I caught Ramon's attention and pointed to her glass. He nodded but rolled his eyes again in disapproval.

"So, what have you found out, Mr. Roddy?" she asked.

"Just Roddy," I said. "I don't want to be in Mr. Freddy's league."

She smiled again, and her smile worked like spontaneous combustion in me.

"What can you tell me of my brother's death?" she said.

Funny thing was, there was no sadness or grief or sense of loss about her brother. Her face conveyed calm, with just a trace of histrionics. She touched the back of my hand with her red fingernails and inhaled deeply so that her tits inflated, affording me a better view. She knew she was working me, I knew she was working me, but beneath the phony allure simmered intrigue.

Ramon brought her another cosmo.

"Tell me, were you and your brother close?" I asked.

She studied a faux Frank Lloyd Wright stained-glass chandelier hanging from the ceiling.

"We were brother and sister," she said, without fanfare.

"I know, but were you close?"

"I am only twenty-five. He was thirty-eight. We had different mothers. We had different views of life. I don't think you could call us close."

"So, tell me again why you're here? Seems like a lot of trouble for someone you weren't close to."

"Like I said, I came to claim my inheritance."

"I'm having trouble understanding."

She lifted the cocktail glass to her wet mouth and sipped, leaving an imprint of lipstick on the rim. She was forever leaving lip prints. I wondered if she had a tattoo of those lips somewhere on her body.

"I told you, I came to speak with Juliano, or I guess I should say Father Juliano, about my inheritance. When I discovered my father had cut me out of his will, I was hoping to convince Juliano to do the Christian thing and give me my share," she said. She ground her cigarette into the glass ashtray already crowded with gold-tipped butts.

She pushed the button on her cigarette case, springing the lid open. She nicked a fresh cigarette from a dwindling row, sparked her gold lighter, and inhaled. She refocused her green eyes on me.

"Your inheritance? How could you inherit from your brother? He was a priest. Don't they take a vow of poverty?"

"Exactly. That's why he didn't need the money," she said. "I'm all for an AIDS hospice. I might even contribute to it. But he stole my half of the estate with lies and deceit, giving me no say about my half of the money."

I played like I didn't know. "AIDS hospice?"

"Yes, he wanted to build an AIDS hospice in Africa. A worthy project, but I had other plans for my inheritance."

"Why did your father cut you out of the will?"

"My father was very provincial, very old-fashioned. My brother convinced him I was…was a slut. That I had no morals. That I was just this side of evil."

At the edge of my vision, I saw a heavy woman in red capris lumbering by, carrying a patent-leather purse. Without warning, she bent over next to me, her butt two ax-handles wide, to straighten out her white socks, but as she went over, she farted. Nicole and I looked at each other, trying not to laugh.

I continued, but in a lighter tone. "Are you a slut?"

Again Nicole smiled. "Wouldn't you like to know."

"Where did you learn your English? It's damn good."

"My dad sent me to some damn good schools, Roddy, and I have a facile tongue," she said. Then she laughed. "For languages."

She tipped her drink and it slid down her throat. The woman could drink.

"I have an idea," she said, without wickedness. "My room for a drink?"

"I don't drink."

"I'll drink for us both. I have a bottle, a glass, some ice. Why pay casino prices? Come on," she said, pushing away from the bar and standing, tugging at the bottom of her bustier, which had risen above her navel. She wore sheer white linen pants that defined every invitation of her haunches. I couldn't detect a panty line or a hint of cellulite. I stood, left money on the bar for Ramon, then followed, enjoying the view of her superbly crafted ass. Just as she had done in the store, she attracted glances. Even women gamblers couldn't resist checking her out.

Once in the room, she kicked off her white high heels. With her, neatness didn't count. Clothes had landed everywhere, on the floor, on the bed, on the desk. A black bra hung like a parachute from the open door of the entertainment center. She squatted in her bare feet and rummaged through the hotel refrigerator, latching onto a three-quarters-full bottle of Stoli. She poured herself a plastic cupful over ice, shoved aside some sweaters and skirts, and sat at the edge of the bed.

"Now what, Roddy?" Her green eyes were playful.

"How much did your brother inherit?"

"Will the questions never end?"

She stood from the bed, gulped her vodka, and reached around behind her back with her right hand. She undid some clasps, then held the bustier against her breasts with her other hand.

"The questions, can't they wait? Isn't there something else we could play?"

She stood appraising me. Then she said, "No, you're right. It isn't fair. All my life I have been told I'm beautiful. I don't know if I am beautiful, but I have had power over men. I could get my way. I like you, Roddy. Liked you right from the start. But I can see you are a man of substance. And I don't want to play you."

She allowed her garment to fall. She walked over to the entertainment center. Her right hand worked on the button of her pants. They fell to the floor as well. It is sometimes said that total nudity is not as sexy as the partially unclad. Nicole exploded that theory.

Then she grabbed a satin robe and wrapped herself in it. Her lush hips still swelled beneath the fabric, but the wantonness was gone.

"What does it matter now?" she said, more to herself than to me. "My brother is dead. I told you maybe I could help with your investigation; I'm going to try. Telling you this feels almost like betrayal, but not quite. I think, in some ways, he had it coming. You see, my brother was sick. He had a thing for young boys. That was how he ended up here in your mission. He was sent here as punishment, as a cover-up, a way of protecting the Church against public outrage. His records are sealed. Even my father didn't know.

But I knew. I knew because I knew a boy he molested before he became a priest. And I heard the later accusations. Yes, my brother molested young boys."

"You're telling me straight?"

I studied her face. Nothing artificial showing. I have a decent bullshit detector. Maybe this was an Oscar-winning performance, but it felt like she was being truthful.

"So did you come here to blackmail your brother into giving you your share of the inheritance?"

"'Blackmail' is an ugly word, but I guess you could say that was my plan. If he didn't willingly give me my inheritance, I would tell Church authorities over here of his past. And it would start all over again, the public shame, the criminal investigations, his excommunication from the Church. He was a paradox. Other than his sexual deviations, he was in all other ways a faithful Catholic. Maybe he thought confession would absolve him of his sins and get him into heaven. I don't know."

She got up, poured herself another drink. She continued: "It isn't easy for me to tell you these things. He was my brother; I share his blood. Sometimes I feel like I share the blame for the vile things he has done. I feel so unclean when I think of him and what he's done. I'm no angel, but I've never done anything so contemptible."

She tipped her glass of straight vodka on the rocks and drained it. She exhaled. Not only breath but spirit left her.

She trained her sad eyes on me and smiled cheerlessly, the kind of absent smile worn when the other girl wins the beauty pageant.

"Now, I feel I have ruined the moment. Maybe when this is all over, you'll come back to see me, Roddy. I feel something building with you I don't often feel. So when this is over, if I haven't ruined it for you, maybe you'll give me a chance, maybe give us a chance?"

And the tears started. And I saw the way she looked when she was five, a young girl who played with dolls and dreamed of armored knights who rode stallions, rescued damsels, and slayed dragons.

I moved toward her, put my arms around her. She buried her face in my neck, her tears warm against my skin, the breath damp on my neck. She sobbed. Between sobs: "What a mess, my life...my brother. May he rot in hell."

I wish I could say I was there only to console, that my every thought was pure. But I could feel her convexities beneath the satin, her body soft yet taut with sexual promise. And I'd be lying if I said I wasn't aroused, if I said I wasn't tempted. But I stopped my hands from tracing the smoothness of her back to the swell of her butt. My breath quickened, my thoughts became desires. But the spell was broken by a tray of room-service dishes dropped onto the floor by the people in the next room. Metal lids clanged against dishes. A glass broke. The mood broke.

I banged on Alex Mendez's door. It was after ten. A working man, he was likely asleep. I banged harder. Biscuits barked. Footsteps advanced. The porch light switched on. The door swung open.

Alex stepped into the light. A big moth bounced against the bulb's glass covering. Other winged insects, drawn by the light, circled around Alex's face like vultures over a carcass. His long hair was in fitful disarray, his eyes swollen, not with sleep but with tears, lids clamped tight against the light, against the world.

"Roddy," he said, his voice quavering, his eyes refusing to meet mine. Angie hid sobbing in the shadows behind him.

"Fish," I said. "Goddamn it, Fish. I'm so sorry, man."

"I know, I know," he said. Then he fell apart. His face folded in on itself, his shoulders heaved, his gut clenched with a wail of such despair it nearly undid me. He looked up at me for help, his eyes like black cauldrons of boiling grief. Being so close to my best friend's pain shattered my heart. This is the life they teach us to say yes to, to be alive to each moment of, but all I wanted was to crawl into oblivion.

Angie, too, keened, falling to her knees, sobbing wildly into her hands, her voice guttural, an almost inhuman growl. Over and over, all she could say was, "Why, God, why?"

Okay, I had come with bad news, but I didn't expect this reaction. I looked at Alex, questions in my eyes.

Alex stepped to the side to let me pass. He pointed to Brian's room. He and Angie rushed toward each other, clinging, both trying to expel horror with their cries.

The door to Brian's room was open. I made my way down the dim hall. The overhead light was on in Brian's room; a chamber of yellow light fell from the open door into the hallway.

I inched into the doorway, fearful of what I'd see.

Alex had set a metal eye into the high Victorian ceiling, bolted it solidly into a brace so it would be good and strong. Alex had hung a water-filled heavy bag on the hook so Brian could punch it. Every thirteen-year-old-boy wanted a knockout punch. Both Alex and I had showed him how to shift forward and turn his hips into the jab to maximize power. We showed him how to level his arm with his elbow and swing with his whole body into a hook. The kid had a natural hook, another Joe Frazier. We showed him how to lead with a jab, and power through with the right cross. We showed him how to come up from a crouch to throw the uppercut. Brian would play James Brown on his bedroom stereo and hit the heavy bag for hours.

But the heavy bag was on the floor leaning into the corner. Brian was hanging from the metal eye, a rope around his neck, his face dark with death. He didn't swing. He didn't move. He didn't anything. His handsome boyish face set into a death mask. His desk chair was kicked onto its side on the floor, next to Brian's shadow. On his desk, a black Bible was opened to Psalm 26. Yellow highlighter marked a passage:

> I hate the assembly of evildoers,
>
> and with the wicked I will not stay.

In the margin Brian had written, *I killed him, but...* before the next words: "I wash my hands in innocence."

The Bible was not a total surprise. Brian was an altar boy who knew religion.

Alex Mendez put another chunk of oak on the sweat fire that heated river rocks to glow. We sat on old wooden chairs left over from the Bureau of Indian Affairs days. Black smoke curled in the dusk, as yellow and orange flames danced around and between the stack of rocks and logs. Wood turned ashen, rocks glowed orange.

How does one heal? How does one survive the death of a child? It had been a month since we buried Brian. Was a month enough time for the living to get on with the business of living?

Alex had seldom left the house since Brian's death. He hadn't worked. He lost fifteen pounds. He moved lifeless, like a robot. His pallid face devoid of joy. The fire cooked the rocks, and I asked the spirit of the rocks: What was the truth of evil? Was it an ungodly force with a will of its own? Did Father Juliano succumb to the devil when he molested Brian? I never believed in a devil, but then I am only certain of my uncertainty. Did Father Juliano act willfully to destroy Brian? Was he powerless to fight his compulsions, or was there an outside force, a Satan, if you will, necessitating the evil?

This was a Luiseño sweat, and Satan, was a Christian construct, but even we pagans acknowledge the existence of evil.

This was a healing sweat, two friends crawling into the womb of Mother Earth looking for solace, for answers, for guidance, for an antidote to a black heart. The world would still be here when we crawled out. So too, I hoped, would Alex's willingness to live.

Me, I didn't get to go trout fishing in Idaho. Nicole hated camping. After the sweat, I would go home to Nicole. She and her lawyer friend, who I never got to meet, were getting closer to sorting out Father Juliano's legal affairs. I knew once she was flush again she'd quickly get bored with my kind of life. She'd jet back to her former self, sunning her wares on the Côte d'Azur, drinking cosmos in Riviera casinos, dancing all night with Armani guys in nightclubs for the jet set. I would be reduced to an anecdote, that Indian guy she'd had a fling with on a real Indian reservation. She'd throw back her head and laugh. "No, silly, they don't live in teepees," she'd say to some Dutch millionaire who wanted to know about reservation life. Besides, I'd had to hire a housekeeper who constantly grumbled about picking up after her. She was indeed a messy houseguest. But I would seize the moment, enjoy it fully while it lasted, knowing it wouldn't last.

She was delicious.

PLATO PLUS ALEXIS

Was it love? Maybe, maybe not. But Plato Peña was a fool for whatever it was. The PLATO PLUS ALEXIS India-ink tattoo he had etched over his heart in eighth grade was proof of that.

Saturday afternoon, with his butt pasted to the San Ignacio Reservation ball field bleachers, Plato read Kahlil Gibran's *The Prophet* while Alexis Palomino, the cherry in his fruit cocktail, hurled for the rez's all-women softball team. Plato didn't pretend to read. He didn't need to pretend. A born multitasker, he could concentrate on the book and ogle Alexis intermittently.

Coastal mountains of sunbaked chamiso and bleached granite surrounded the San Ignacio ball field that was formerly a cow pasture. The ball field's weathered bleachers bowed beneath the weight of heavy Indian backsides. Indian cars—rusting gas hogs with doughnut-smooth tires, coat hangers for antennas, official INDIAN CAR bumper stickers—were parked outside the ballpark fence of bailing wire strung between dead tree limbs.

Alexis, known for her curveball and her curves, posed on the mound, cleats on the rubber, kneading the softball in her glove, long black hair in a braid. San Ignacio cap backward, tight purple-sleeved jersey, gray sliding pants sprayed on, eyes trained on the catcher's mitt.

It was late August, summer strumming its last chords, but hot enough to force dogs to hunt shade. The slanting sun whitewashed the sky and profiled Alexis in long shadows on the infield grass. Even her shadow was *Playboy*-worthy.

No one but Plato, oddball that he was, read in the bleachers. Others came to enjoy the game, socialize, and watch Alexis. Almost six foot, she had the height and leverage to windmill the ball with incredible speed and accuracy. Fresh out of high school, she was blossoming as a rez legend. "Maybe she'll play college ball," people said over morning eggs and beans, though not too loud out of fear it might jinx her. The jinx felled too many Indian athletes for it to be simple coincidence; too many natural athletes idled under pepper trees, a bottle of Thunderbird substituting for achievement. Some thought it the Indian curse.

Alexis came by her abilities genetically. Her father, a towering Lakota, played inspired basketball, all elbows and aerial grace under the backboards. Several years ago, though, in drunken despondency over pancreatic cancer, he overdosed on sleeping pills. His suicide left Alexis an orphan. Her mother, a former powwow princess in her own right, had died of a burst appendix when Alexis was five. But father and mother left behind a good measure of grit in their daughter. Alexis was a tough girl, a helluva softball player. On top of that, a helluva good-looking softball player. Men joked that the rule books should be changed to call her safe when her tits got to the base before the ball did.

It was hard for Plato to even look at Alexis, her beauty generated such heat in him. To avoid staring, which could lead to embarrassment, he held *The Prophet*'s pages open against the rustling Pacific breeze.

Plato was nerdy. People often wisecracked about his Coke-bottle lenses, his slack-shouldered stoop, his lack of coordination. He shrugged off the insults because he had no choice. He needed glasses. Years of reading in bad light had weakened his eyes. People joked that masturbation may have contributed, but he didn't buy into that whole theory. He couldn't change his walk, couldn't fix his stoop. Maybe he could have built up his shoulders, but he detested exercise. Instead, he read Gibran: "When you work you are a flute through whose heart the whispering of the hours turns to music."

Plato had an ear for Gibran's music, but he was more than a little ashamed of it. If people knew what he was reading, he'd get a ration of shit for sure. But hell with it. The words soothed him, a calming countermeasure to Alexis's physical effect on him. Anyway, it was a safe bet nobody at the game had read or even heard of Gibran. Most thought Plato an egghead, so it probably wouldn't surprise them to know what he was reading. "Weird," they'd say with a shake of the head. "The boy is weird."

If you asked Porterhouse, the beefy guy in the Dodgers T-shirt sitting two rows down, he'd say Plato was weird. But really, he didn't give Plato much thought. Porterhouse reached into a Styrofoam cooler between his feet and retrieved an icy can of Coors. He popped the top, tipped back his head, and poured the beer down his open throat. Fat bunched up on the back of his neck like a pack of hot dogs, little flesh tags dangling off the creased skin like swollen ticks. In his day, Porterhouse had been an MVP shortstop, but that was thirty years and ten thousand beers ago. These days he was content to be on life's sidelines, a spectator to goings-on with beer-fogged eyes.

"Hum it in there, girl," he hollered, his voice sandpapered by Marlboros. Then under his breath he said, "Man, would I like to hum on her." The beer distorted his sense of volume, and he said it loud enough for others, including Plato, to hear. Plato's teeth clenched at the words. Men were always saying stuff about Alexis; he couldn't get used to it. He hadn't figured out how to handle this part of the Alexis dream. Her obvious bounty drew so many stares and crude comments that Plato might be in a fight every day. And Plato, by philosophy, was a pacifist. Plus, he was a lousy fighter. Tall and thin, too gangly to deliver much of a haymaker, Plato had spent his life sidestepping fisticuffs. He sat silent, loose hair tickling his right cheek, sipping Pepsi on ice from a waxed-paper cup, swallowing the carbonated cola with his pride.

"Don't be so rude, Porterhouse, she's just a young girl," said Plato's grandmother, Polly, who sat next to Plato.

Porterhouse craned his fat neck back to look at her. "What? I didn't say nuthin'."

"Keep it that way. She's too young for your dirty-old-man mind."

That got the bleacher bunch chuckling and Porterhouse turned toward the game, slightly reddened. And Porterhouse didn't shame easily.

"Tell him, Gram," Plato whispered.

His grandmother, who knew things about Plato he didn't suspect she knew, patted his knee. Plato was over 6 foot 7, his knees nearly touching his chin as he sat on the sagging bleacher bench. And he really was skinny. Ribs and sinew showed through his long-sleeved T-shirt. Indian boys his age often wore muscle shirts to show off rippling triceps. Plato preferred to hide his twigs beneath long sleeves. He had respectable long hair, though, that snaked to his shoulders. But his heavy tortoiseshell glasses bit into his crooked beak, rendering his magnified eyes perpetually astonished. Plato's peepers jitterbugged behind thick glass.

Indians from reservations all over the Southland loaded their kids into pickups and cars and headed to the diamond for the

Saturday afternoon games. Older folks took the bleacher seats. The younger crowd stood in clusters along the fence and in between cars, drinking beer and swapping stories. Horns, those that worked, honked at home runs and outstanding plays. Backers whistled and screamed encouragement. Adding to the tumult, black crows cawed in overhead flybys, eyes peeled for a dropped tortilla roll or spilled popcorn. The afternoon chugged on as people got buzzed. They passed the hat to make more beer runs.

San Ignacio regulars filled the stands. Take, for instance, Dora, a woman in a pink puffed-out muumuu that half-covered ankles thick as cheese rounds. She stood and screamed, "Come on, San Ignacio. You got this!" She plopped back down and returned to her bean-and-hamburger tortilla roll. She dined refined, like European royalty, her pinky outstretched as if sipping tea from Dresden china. She nipped a dainty bite of tortilla roll and chewed like a Barbie doll. But there wasn't much of Dora that was Barbie-like. Dora was better known on the rez as Bomber. She celebrated her proportions, full of belly laughs, always smiling. Despite her weight, the woman could dance. At a party, after a couple of swigs of T-Bird, she'd give Chuck Berry hell, bumping and grinding, belting out "Johnny B. Goode" loud enough to drown the mission bells. Good luck to any unsuspecting man she lured into her clutches. She was known to leave hapless thrill-seekers desiccated of juices, little more than transparent husks stuck on the spiderweb. Plato had known Dora all his life. He didn't lift his eyes from the page to say hello or acknowledge her. He'd sat next to her, with his grandmother on the other side of him. Dora didn't feel snubbed. She'd known Plato all his life too.

Funny how Plato could focus on a book with the commotion of a softball game whirling about him. His word-fixated eyes crinkled at the corners as his mind locked on to meaning and drowned out all else. All his life, Plato found connection in books. Not only did they keep the outside world at bay, they alerted him to his own inner workings. "Love has no other desire but to fulfill itself," wrote Gibran. Plato loved books.

"Steeeerrrriiikkke!" the umpire hollered. "You're outta here!"

Alexis had fanned another hitter to retire the side. San Ignacio fans whooped, and the team charged into the dugout for their ups as the Soboba team ran out onto the field. Plato glanced up from the page to watch Alexis run. He couldn't miss that. He smiled at her satisfied smile as she trotted to the dugout. He lingered a moment, appreciating her jigglies, then refocused on the page: "Where shall you seek beauty, and how shall you find her unless she herself be your way and your guide?"

Plato's grandmother never missed a home game, and Plato tagged along to watch Alexis. For added comfort, Polly carried her own padded seat complete with backrest that fitted to the bleacher. In an insulated game bag that Plato had gotten her two Christmases ago, she brought a handful of sugar-free chocolates and a six-pack of Fresca, her main drink since being diagnosed diabetic. They didn't sell Fresca out of the bathtub of ice in the snack bar. Should the game get a little slow, why she'd pop open a Fresca and whip out her book of crossword puzzles. If she didn't know a four-letter word for sodium chloride, she could ask Plato. He'd know. He knew most everything.

"Are you excited?" she asked.

"About?"

"About Stanford tomorrow, silly."

"Yes, I guess." Plato had graduated from high school in June. He was still seventeen. He had a huge vocabulary, the highest ever recorded at his high school, but like most teens, natural-born sullenness precluded wordiness with adults. Even his grandmother didn't get much conversation.

"Are you all packed?"

"Just about."

"Make sure you pack that scarf your mother knitted for you. It would hurt her something awful if you didn't take it." Polly scratched her permed gray hair with plain fingernails, flecks of dandruff floating to her shoulders.

"Yeah, yeah, yeah. I will." That's what Plato said, but he thought otherwise. He wanted to say, "Like she didn't hurt me when she took off with that rat-bastard Washoe man to Gardnerville and left me here without even a picture to remember her by?" But his grandmother was one to whitewash family graffiti. In her world, families got along; everybody did right by each other. At least, that's the way she wanted her world to be, and she chose not to recognize when it was otherwise.

Plato, ever the realist, figured no matter how thick the coat of paint, the dirty words remained beneath. But it would do no good to bring his mother up now. Resurrecting past hurts would sound petulant. He wanted to consider himself, and to be considered by others, a man. Tomorrow he would be on a bus for Palo Alto, headed for the ivy halls of academia. He was gonna be a Stanford Cardinal. Excited? Hell yes. His whole life had been an arrow aimed at college.

Polly knew Plato stewed over his mother's abrupt departure. She knew her daughter had done wrong, but Polly didn't speak of it. She loved her daughter. She loved Plato. She was a fixer. She'd persevere, dammit. Every morning, after Mass, she prayed in the mission chapel. She prayed for the repose of the soul of her husband, dead of a heart attack now fifteen years. She prayed for her daughter, Maxine—no matter how naughty she was—that she was safe and happy. She prayed Plato could overcome the sour taste of abandonment. She prayed for happy endings.

Yes, Maxine had always been a wild child. Plato, and his sister, Leela, were the fruits of her impulses, babies born of disregard for consequences. Polly had long acknowledged that she would forever pay dues for her daughter's excesses. But maybe, she weighed, it was her fault. If she had been a better mother, maybe her daughter would have been different. The sins of her own youth prompted sins in Maxine, and so it passed from generation to generation, she thought. She was doing her best with Plato, trying to right some wrongs.

Sheila Sanchez, the center fielder, waited on a slow curve and lined it to right field. She rounded first and held up as Soboba's right fielder rifled the ball to the cutoff. Alexis, on deck, banged her bat against steel cleats and strode over to the batter's box. Many players wore the newer plastic cleats, but Alexis preferred old-school metal. She figured they gave her better traction on the mound. Plus, infielders tended to get out of her way when she was sliding.

Alexis threw righty but batted lefty. She dug her cleats in, bent her knees, jutted out her rump, and waved the bat like a war club, high off her left shoulder. She was relaxed in her stance, shifting her weight, front to back, as the pitcher wound up and fired. Fastball. Low and inside. "Ball one," blue called.

Plato's eyes lifted from the page. He loved Alexis's batting stance. It suggested endless possibilities. Plato studied the musculature of her thighs, rejoiced at the roundness of her haunches, mused over her sculpted back, her single black braid splitting it into symmetrical halves. Plato couldn't see her breasts as she leaned over the plate, but he imagined all right. No doubt about it, her body was custom-made for athletics, and other delights. Sure, Plato was still a virgin. But he had a stack of men's magazines a foot and a half high hidden in a shed out back. He admired feminine pulchritude, and Alexis had it in aces. No girlie photo he'd ever seen bettered her, which reminded him to hide the magazines in a safer place before leaving for Stanford. Plato took another look at Alexis leaning over the plate, then resumed *The Prophet*: "We have seen her leaning over the earth from the windows of the sunset." That sentence was way too appropriate for that particular moment, Plato thought. Was it a sign?

A couple of pitches later, Plato was engrossed in the lines "And beauty is not a need but an ecstasy. It is not a moth thirsting nor an empty hand stretched forth, but rather a heart enflamed and a soul enchanted." It was midway through that passage that Alexis watched her foul ball rocket above the backstop and drop onto the crown of Plato's head, exactly in the cranial depression that, if he were still a baby, would be called his "soft spot." She winced at the thud of horsehide against skull.

Plato's eyes spun and he spilled forward onto the back of Willa Sanchez, the center fielder's mother. Willa had stood to avoid the plummeting ball, and the impact of Plato's lurching body knocked her off balance, tumbling her onto Leroy Toney, a man in his eighties, who fell like a domino into Cathy Hyde, in front of him. Luckily, her three hundred pounds remained stable, and the toppling ended there. But Willa had spilled her beer onto Leroy's khaki shirt, and the impact of Willa into Leroy caused his upper dentures to spit from his mouth onto the ground beneath the bleachers.

The tip of Plato's tongue had been resting between his teeth while he was reading, and the brunt of the softball, which really wasn't so soft, knocked his teeth through his tongue. Not only was he sprawled unconscious on the bleacher plank in front of him, his mouth spurted blood like a hemophiliac slit with a straight razor.

Polly emitted a short outburst of alarm: "Plato?" She hurried to him, hoping to get him upright. That's when she saw the blood seeping from his mouth. Others exclaimed, Dora almost fainted, and someone hollered for a doctor. Polly didn't panic. A former nurse's aide and veteran of child-rearing trenches, she'd seen blood before. She pried apart his clamped teeth and saw blood streaming from his gashed tongue. At least it's not internal, she thought. She grabbed ice from his Pepsi cup and rubbed his face with it. Plato's eyes fluttered into consciousness and he groaned.

She slipped more ice into his mouth once he fully came to.

"What the hell happened?" he asked.

"Foul ball conked you on the noggin," Polly said.

"Man, it felt like an anvil crashed onto my skull."

"Nope. Just a softball," she said. Careful not to slight his manhood, she added, "But it came down hard."

The ice slowed the bleeding, but he still swallowed cold blood. His head hurt. His tongue stung. His chin was scraped where it had clipped the bleachers.

"I hope I don't have a concussion. I can't see. My eyes are all blurry."

"Your glasses fell off."

Instinctively, he felt for his horn-rims. Sure enough, they were gone.

"Bobby," Polly hollered to a small boy who was standing at the backstop laughing at Plato with his friends. "Bobby, I'll give you a dollar to get Plato's glasses. They're on the ground."

"Get my teeth too," Leroy said.

"You gonna give me a dollar?" Bobby said.

"Well, hell, you little sonof—"

Polly interrupted: "I'll give you another dollar. Get Leroy's teeth, Bobby."

Bobby circled around to the underside of the bleachers. Mostly, kids weren't allowed under the bleachers. Women knew they ducked under there to peek up dresses. When he crawled under, Bobby couldn't resist looking up either, to see what he could see. He took his sweet time but eventually found the false teeth and Plato's glasses.

$\int$an Ignacio beat Soboba five to one—Soboba's only run scored on fielding errors. Alexis had pitched a one-hitter. She swung by the bleachers on her way out, her fielder's glove tucked beneath her armpit, her eyes brimming with victory. Polly, busy gathering her ball-game accessories, didn't notice her approach. Plato was reading, sucking on ice. Polly had given him a couple of aspirin from her purse, and his pounding head had quieted to a dull ache.

"You okay?" Alexis shouted up to Plato, hand on her hip like a calendar girl, her head tilted provocatively up at him. Plato and Alexis had gone to school together since kindergarten. But had she ever talked directly to him before? Oh, maybe when she called him pantywaist, or gomer, or snot-eater. Yeah, she caught him eating snot at his desk in second grade. "Eeeeuuuwww," she had wailed. Plato had tried to shrink inside himself, to disappear. He had always been too absorbed in other things to be much good at social graces. Without thinking, he still fingered his nose at times in the middle of a lengthy paragraph. But here, after a lifetime of put-downs and disregard, Alexis Palomino was standing before him, a smudge of dirt on her right cheek, asking about his well-being. One for the record books.

Plato froze. Only his eyes moved, blinking like a pinfeathered pigeon behind his glasses.

"Answer her," whispered his grandmother, jabbing him with an elbow.

"Um, er, I'm good," he said, his tongue still thick.

"Good. I was hoping I didn't kill you," Alexis said. "Probably not a good idea to read during games."

"Yeah, I guess," Plato said, his head dropping half an inch in shame.

"Say, a bunch of us are headed for the racetrack in a few, if you're up for it," Alexis said.

Was she inviting him to the racetrack? Was the world spinning off its axis?

"Uh, yeah, sure," he said.

"Cool. See you there, then." She smiled and strolled off, her long legs sanctifying the ground she walked on.

"I don't think you should go," Polly said, as she slung her game bag onto the Formica kitchen table.

"I have to," he said. Plato had seldom been invited anywhere before. To show up would mean something. He wasn't quite sure what it would mean. But he had to go. Alexis was expecting him. To back out now would be chickenshit.

"But your head?"

"I'm okay, really."

"But there will be drinking down there. I've heard what goes on. Your Uncle Peter comes for you at six a.m. You don't want to miss your Greyhound for college."

"I know, Gram. I'll be ready."

"That girl is trouble."

"What?"

"I don't know what she wants, but she wants something. I don't trust her."

Polly's glare bore through Plato's lenses at his astonished man-child eyes. Plato put his hand on top of the refrigerator and leaned against it.

"Gram," Plato said, his shoulders raised in exasperation.

"I'm telling you, she's up to no good. She's too fast for you."

"Thanks, Gram, you're a real confidence-builder."

"It's for your own good. You know I'm right."

Funny thing is, Plato knew his grandmother was probably right, but the call of the wild was too strong.

The evening light turned syrupy purple out the kitchen window. The refrigerator kicked on. Plato yanked it open and snagged a leftover pork chop. He took a bite and chewed, looking at his grandmother. Wrinkles etched the loose skin behind her gold-rimmed glasses. He noted the deepening folds at the upturn of her lips, and he noted the sun-ravaged skin protruding from her paisley blouse. The kitchen clock, a dime-store Westclox plugged into a socket just above the table, ticked like a metronome counting beats of his life. Plato turned, headed out the front door into dusk. His dog, Frosty, a kinky-haired Airedale, fell into step at his heels.

Polly went to the front window and watched Plato walk the dirt road toward the river. He walked loose, like a rubber man, like a Great Dane puppy. And for a second, she saw him as a toddler, crying, running toward her, his diaper drooping with a full load. Fear choked her, fear for her grandson, who was more like a son, and she bit the inside of her cheek to ward it off. Who was going to protect him from cruelty, especially as he walked out of her life and into his own? She must have faith—faith that he had enough wiles to survive. She had to believe, because if she didn't, what else was there?

Tucked amid brushy hills across the San Luis Rey River, the racetrack had been the brainchild of some entrepreneurial Indian a decade or more before—a dirt track for motocross races. But few outsiders could ever find the damn track it was so far back in the brush. It failed as a business but succeeded as a place to hang out. The track stayed, and rez youths raced their old trucks and dirt bikes in those hills, far enough from the village so no one complained. In the night, teens often circled their cars, lit a bonfire in the center, and partied till the booze ran out. No one complained much about that either. Better to have them on the reservation, people thought, than to have them messing up on city streets. No telling what trouble they'd find there.

Plato hoofed his way toward the track, following a path that wove between shifting shadows of sage chamise and scrub oak. Sleeping quail blundered from a sugar-bush as Frosty bounded into their scent, stub of a tail beating the air. Night descending, the air turned velvety.

Plato covered distance quickly, his long-legged gait eating up geography, but it was a forty-five-minute walk. Beads of sweat collected at his hairline, and his breath came in steam-engine bursts. Plato didn't smoke, but he was badly out of shape. He was hopeless in P.E. Archery saved him. He could outshoot anybody in the school with a bow. He could hit a Ping-Pong ball at twenty paces every time. But archery was a dork sport. Might as well play tuba in the marching band. He suffered the terrible shame that he couldn't hit a jump shot to save his life. His older sister, Leela, a senior at Arizona State, starred as a ball-handling forward. Leela could play. The two of them grew up with a dirt court and hoop out back. Plato tried. He tried and tried, practiced hours and hours, but he threw up bricks that banged against the rim or air balls that bounced into the bougainvillea.

If he could have played basketball, his popularity would have been guaranteed. Indians respected basketball. Man, if only he could play, things would be so different. How could Leela be so good at b-ball when he was so bad? They both had height. But Leela's father was good at sports. He was real good at pool and ran off to hustle tables in skid-row Los Angeles. Eventually, he was stabbed by a Mexican guy over a pool game in a downtown bar. At least that's the story Polly heard from Eddie Montoya, who said he saw the whole thing happen.

Nobody was sure who Plato's father was. Maxine may have known, but she never said. Plato grew up fatherless in a household of women, so isolated from men that he'd never even seen a man shave. Luckily, he didn't have enough facial hair for it to matter. He learned about masculinity from books and from high school teachers. Teachers and Hemingway characters became his role models. Because Plato was smart, teachers had always taken a liking to him. He tried to stay unnoticed, and seldom raised his hand to answer questions in class. He knew classmates would think him an obnoxious know-it-all if he fired off his intellect in class. No matter how hard he tried to be invisible, the teachers found him. Soon he'd be teacher's pet, providing more ammunition for wisecracking classmates.

School was bad, but it wasn't much better at home, growing up. Polly was always great, but his mom and his sister—yikes. He knew the full meaning of PMS. He had coat-hanger scars to prove it. His mother had a nasty temper, so Plato learned early to stay out of her way. He hid beneath the bed and in books as a toddler. In books, he was a million miles away. He taught himself to read before he was three. Books were his best friends, really his only friends. His penchant for reading earned him his nickname, Plato. Plato's real name was Paul, but people had long forgotten it. It was his mother who first called him Plato, but she'd said it derisively, as a way of poking fun. Why did he still miss her? Am I stupid? he thought. He knew he wasn't stupid, though. He'd scored a perfect 1600 on the SATs, the only Indian student to ever do it at his school. And once in a while, his mother could be nice, like when she made him cornbread. To this day, he loved her cornbread, especially the way she made it with jalapeños and cheese and real corn kernels in a cast-iron skillet. Even his grandmother couldn't make cornbread as good as Maxine.

When Plato hit the top of the hill overlooking the racetrack, the first thing he heard in the sandy swale below was a roaring V8. Doug "Freaky" Friday spun doughnuts in his souped-up Road Runner. Dust rooster-tailed in gritty billows as he slid in circles, his engine roaring, his car bucking through the ruts. A bonfire of pallets and oak branches lit the sky a smarmy orange. Plato thought he could make out Mary Wells's "My Guy" blaring from a car stereo. A girl's laugh, shrill as a cartoon witch's, cut the night. As soon as he heard it, Plato knew Downtown Adele Brown was there.

Plato stood and surveyed the scene. Kids, about ten of them, kids he'd gone to school with, kids he'd been ignored by, kids he'd been rejected by his whole life, waited below. He pulled up short, his weight shifting to one leg in hesitation. Did he really want to mingle with those assholes? Did he want to eat shit one more night as if it were a goodbye present to take with him to Stanford?

Plato closed his eyes and saw himself twenty years from now. He'd have a doctorate in philosophy, be guest lecturing at the Sorbonne, dining afterward in a Left Bank restaurant, drinking wine and exchanging witticisms with the French intelligentsia. He'd be with people who admired and understood his intelligence. They wouldn't care if he couldn't hit a jump shot. Did his dreams of the future make him less Indian? In twenty years, Doug "Freaky" Friday would be doing exactly what he was doing now, pumping out shithouses for a Valley Center sanitation company. Then he'd come home to argue with his wife over rent money blown in bars and bingo halls. Did that make Doug more Indian? Did being Indian require an absence of ambition?

Plato needed more out of life, maybe because he'd always felt unwanted. Every day, he had sat alone in the San Ignacio Mission School cafeteria, suffocated by lime-green walls, washing down mushy meatloaf with milk souring in a waxed carton. No one ever came up to him: "Can I join you, Plato?" "Mind if I sit with you, Plato?" "What's that you're reading, Plato?"

The playground was a worse hell. As a first-grader, he didn't know he didn't fit in. He'd tried to scramble across the monkey bars with the other kids. But the other kids had spotted his peculiarities right off. He still had a scar on his forehead from where he'd crashed face-first into the asphalt after Arnie Archuletta scissored him with spring-steel legs, yanking Plato's grip loose, smacking him into the ground. Each day, Plato sat on a bench against the school wall near the merry-go-round and read while other kids spun themselves sick. Humiliation smothered him, made him struggle for every breath.

Alexis was part of it. Mostly she ignored him. But she often collaborated, even initiated the razzing at times. He should hate her, but fat chance of that. He cared for her from the beginning, from the first time he saw her, even before she got tits.

She came to school, her bobby socks rolled down to the tops of her black-and-white saddle shoes, sassy and smart-mouthed. She liked lavender-colored pens, and even though she was right-handed, she did her cursive in a loopy back slant. She chewed Doublemint gum nonstop in class, but the nuns never told her to spit it out. She was too damn cute for discipline. Because both he and Alexis were tall, and because both were born on Christmas Day, Plato figured they had to be soul mates of sorts.

He was hopeless, but she was mean to him. And that hurt even more. He never imagined anyone else for himself, though. Neither could he imagine Alexis ever being with him. He had a better chance of curing cancer than being with Alexis, he thought.

About two hundred yards away, Alexis leaned against a Chevy truck, her foot on the bumper. The leaping fire pumped a corona of light into the night. A half-dozen parked cars circled the fire.

Can of Coors in her hand, she squeezed it into an hourglass shape, a nervous habit. She also peeled labels off bottled beer. Girlfriends laughed and told her she was sexually frustrated. Maybe so, she thought. Maybe so. But her girlfriends would shit a brick if they knew the truth.

Beer got her in trouble. She'd started on beer when she was about fifteen. On the afternoon following her father's funeral, she'd lifted a case of Coors from the back of a beer delivery truck as the driver restocked inside the San Ignacio Store. Alexis, and her catcher, Philomena Notros, carted the beer to an abandoned house and downed the whole case. Phena, as they called her, blew chunks in the corner of the house. But it turned out Alexis could handle her suds. What she couldn't handle was her father's death.

She figured drinking helped her to share her father's burden. From the day he died, she carried his church key like a nun with a rosary. No matter how many beers she drank, one or twenty-one, it tasted like the beer her father let her swig when she was a toddler. It tasted of her father's kisses, brought him close, like the smell of Old Spice cologne, like the way his work boots felt on her feet when she tried to dance the hokey pokey in them. But she drank too much. She knew it.

Plato could see Alexis, bathed in firelight and dust, chugging her beer. Doug, stupid Doug, was still spinning brodies, kicking up dust. Plato knew Doug and Alexis had something going. Doug was three years older and could drink in bars. He'd taken her into a few. Plato had heard rumors that Doug wanted to marry Alexis. He'd heard that when he asked her, she just gulped beer till her eyes watered.

Alexis watched, with a sinking heart, as Doug spun circles in the dirt, laughing like an idiot.

Alexis shook her head and withered against the truck. "Are you okay, girl?" Phena asked. A strand of black hair was stuck in the corner of Alexis's mouth, and Phena plucked it out with a thumb and forefinger. Alexis jumped. She didn't hear Phena above the noise from stupid Doug's car.

Phena moved closer, repeating her question.

"What?" Alexis asked. "Yeah, yeah, I'm just dandy." Her voice quavered.

"I don't know what, but something's been bothering you," Phena said.

"I'm okay, really," Alexis said. "I'm good. I'm good."

"Are you and Doug okay? He hasn't been shitting on you has he?"

"Nobody shits on me, Phena. You know that. Now let me drink in peace."

Alexis shifted her head to look at Phena. Although Alexis's words brimmed with bravado, her eyes pleaded for something. Phena thought she simply wanted to be alone, and slid over to where Shorty sat. It didn't work to push Alexis.

Alexis grimaced, her stained-glass gaze searching the flames for an escape.

*P*lato, taking a deep breath, forced himself to walk into the firelight. About four girls and six guys, all friends of Alexis, looked at him like he was an alien invader. Someone threw an empty bottle at a granite boulder and it shattered with a pop. Doug finally stopped spinning; maybe he was running low on gas. The music had changed to Brenton Wood's "I Think You've Got Your Fools Mixed Up."

"Plato? Hey, goddamn it, Plato's here," shouted Shorty, jumping up from the old tractor tire he sat on. "Jesus, Plato, what the hell, are you lost?"

Plato ignored Shorty. He was no particular friend. For a laugh, in fourth grade Shorty had dumped a cup of crushed ice down Plato's shirt while they were in line before class. As Plato shimmied to get the ice out, the kids howled and shouted scarecrow jokes, since *The Wizard of Oz* had been on TV the night before. Sister Mary Daniels thought Plato was clowning on purpose. She made him write a hundred times: "I will march like a Christian soldier while in line."

Alexis spotted Plato. "You made it!" she said to Plato, and walked over to him, smiling at him, like he was somebody.

What the hell is she up to? Plato wondered.

She looked sharply at Shorty. "I invited him," she said. Shorty shrugged.

She took him by the arm closer to the fire. Firelight dallied in her pupils, her purple eye shadow deepening their luster. A waterfall of black hair shimmered to the small of her back. Gold hoop earrings shimmied from her earlobes every time she moved her head. Glossy red lipstick liquefied her lips. A low-cut spaghetti-strap blouse accentuated her positives. Voltage sparked from her hand into his arm. Her slightest touch unleashed tidal waves that banged his ribcage.

"Can I get you a beer, Plato?"

"I don't drink."

"Ah, come on, just one."

"No thanks."

Alexis's brows furrowed. "What the hell..." She stopped herself. "Good for you, Plato. Good for you."

Alexis looked around the fire. Her friends, including Phena,

Mercy, and Sheila—all players on the team—stood in clutches whispering, shooting Alexis incredulous glances. What the hell was she doing with that loser, Plato?

Alexis continued unconcerned. She took big swallows of her beer, gulping till nothing but foam lingered at the bottom. She bent for a bottle, this time from a cardboard case, prying off the cap with the church key attached to the belt loop of her Levi's cutoffs. Her purple fingernail polish was peeled and cracked, but Plato couldn't care less. He sucked in his breath. To be this close, in the night, in the firelight...She was Beauty absolute. He felt stirrings and worried a erection might tent his jeans.

To deflate his arousal, he pictured Dora, naked, eating a vanilla wedding cake. But Plato was seventeen, an age where mental powers have little chance against hormones. Alexis noticed the uprising. There was no denying it.

"I'm glad you came, Plato," Alexis said. "I wondered if you would." She looked different somehow. Her facial muscles had softened. Was that kindness in her eyes? This wasn't the Alexis who'd cracked a rotten hen's egg on his head in third grade. Plato shrugged. Unsure of what to say, he said nothing.

"I asked you here because I want to say something to you, Plato. I know I've been shitty to you. But I'm trying to change all that. I want to say I'm sorry."

Plato couldn't believe his ears. Alexis wasn't the type to apologize. Not to Plato, not to anybody. What the hell was going on?

"I'm trying to change my ways, Plato. Raising hell with you was mean. I don't want to be that way anymore," Alexis said. He wanted to believe her. But he had doubts. Was she going to pour beer on him, trip him so he fell in the fire, call her friends over and have him beat up? That would be more like Alexis.

Over by the fire, Roach, a strange, elfin-sized guy who was

a lightning-fast guard on the basketball court, lit a dried willow branch in the fire and put it to his crotch to make it look like he had a flaming penis. He turned to Phena. "Look, Phena, I'm on fire for you. Think you could blow me out?"

"Not even in your wet dreams, Bug Boy," she said, but laughed after she said it.

Neither Plato nor Alexis paid attention to them. The two stood intent on each other.

"Why should I trust you?" Plato asked, matter-of-factly, in a voice he hardly recognized.

"You're right. I don't see how you can. But I wish you would, because I have something to ask you."

"Here it comes," Plato said. "There had to be a catch." But he was secretly pleased with himself for at least conversing with Alexis.

Alexis measured him with calculating eyes. How should she handle this? For a second, Alexis felt control of the conversation and of Plato slipping away. She decided on a different bait.

She tugged him away from the fire into the darkness, away from invasive eyes, back behind the truck. She sat on the lowered tailgate, her legs swinging, her frayed shorts inching up her golden thigh. She pulled Plato close to her. He could smell the beer on her breath, the fire smoke in her hair, the hint of perfume behind her ears.

"Do you like me, Plato? Don't answer that. I can see that you like me. I think you've had a crush on me since we were kids. Have you?"

"Every guy with eyes has a crush on you, Alexis. I'm nothing special in that regard."

Yes, he was talking to her. He was stating his opinion. He couldn't believe this was his own mouth, his own voice at work. Something surged in Plato. It was as if he didn't care anymore; he was so tired of being shit on.

"Cut to the chase, Alexis, why did you ask me down here? If it's jostled in lazy whitecaps, sun glinting off the blue-gray surface. Alexis sat in the window seat, nodding to the beat of Marvin Gaye playing from a small cassette player wired to her ears. Plato sat next to her, folded into the seat that only reclined an inch when he pressed the recline button. He was finishing up Gibran but had James Joyce's *Dubliners* ready. Between them, resting partly on her thigh, partly on his, was a grocery bag of roasted peanuts that Polly had sent along for the trip. At first Polly had flipped when she'd heard Alexis was going. But her motherly instinct took over when she had heard why.

Looking straight ahead, Alexis removed one of the cassette player's earphones.

"I don't know what's going to happen, Plato," she said, not looking at him.

He put down the book and looked at her. "No one does."

"I don't know if I can go through with the abortion," she said.

"I don't blame you," Plato said. "It's a tough call. All you can do think it through, and then decide with your heart."

"Maybe I don't have a heart," she said.

"But then, maybe you do," he said.

They both reached into the peanut bag at the same time. In the g, their fingers touched, lingering longer than necessary.

---

to humiliate me further, don't bother. I've hit bottom," Plato said, in an antagonistic voice so unlike him. He'd crossed over into the danger zone. She could whistle and Dwayne and Doug and Roach and a couple of other guys would come over and pound the crap out of him. Hell, she could probably whip him on her own. She was strong, an athlete, and had been in fights. The only fight he'd ever won was the grappling match against a stubborn package of Hostess Twinkies, and that was hard fought.

Alexis frowned at him. "Plato, don't be that way."

"Why am I here? You, your whole bunch, has never done anything but torment me. Why am I here? Haven't you had enough fun at my expense? Wasn't seventeen years of it enough?" Plato's chest heaved. His words edged through his teeth.

"Calm down, Plato. Calm down and I'll tell you."

Plato looked off at the hills. He wasn't gonna cry, was he? He couldn't cry. Not here. Not now.

"I know you're going to Stanford tomorrow."

"Yeah?"

"So here's the deal. I want you to take me with you."

"What?"

"Yeah, I want you to take me with you. It's no big deal. Just let me ride with you on the bus. Show me the ropes. I've been saving money, enough for a bus ticket and then some. Pick me up on your way out and take me with you. You're smart. You know your way around. I've hardly ever been off this reservation. So I'm scared to leave on my own. I'm being honest, Plato, no bullshit. I'm scared. But if I don't get outta here, if I don't get away, I'll be stuck here. I'll wither and die here, Plato."

Plato looked at her, his mouth open, his eyes squinting with doubt.

She continued: "I'm a ballplayer, Plato. I don't have your brains.

I didn't get the grades or the test scores for Stanford, or anywhere else. But I'm not stupid, and I could make it in college if I worked real hard. I have dreams too, Plato."

Tears started to trickle down her cheek. Her lips twisted. "I don't want to spend the rest of my life playing rez ball, getting drunk after games, living a nowhere life. I need a chance at something bigger, Plato. You can help me."

"Me? What can I do? I'm nothing. You and your crew have made that clear."

"I was wrong. We were wrong. If I could take it all back, I would, Plato. Just take me with you. My suitcase is packed," she said.

Plato looked at the mascara-blackened tears of this girl who had pissed on him all these years. Anger welled up again. No way. If I let her, this girl will use me till the day I die. Use me up and toss me away. Listen to your grandmother, he thought. She's up to no good.

"I don't think so, Alexis. If you wanna go, why don't you just go? You don't need me," Plato said.

"Because I'm scared, goddamn it. I do need you. You don't know how I need you. You have me all wrong, Plato. I was mean to you, I know it. But did you ever think I was jealous of you?"

"Jealous?"

"Yeah, jealous. I admired you, your smarts, how your life was going somewhere. I wished I could be more like you. You have a brain. You have a direction. You're going to college. You're gonna be somebody."

"What are you talking about, Alexis? You're the most beautiful woman on the planet. You have a great pitching arm. You're the one who's gonna make it."

"I want to, but I need help to get outta here," Alexis said. She bit her underlip and looked about five years old. A protective urge flashed in Plato.

Divided, Plato stood motionless. But no, he wouldn't be made a fool of again. He had to change too. Be stronger. He said, "Get Doug to help you." He half turned to walk away.

Then she shouted: "Don't make me beg, you bastard!" And sh[e] slapped him with her right hand, the one with her CLASS OF '78 rin[g] on it. Plato's cheek stung and turned red with her handprint. Fro[m] standing at Plato's right leg, stiffened and growled.

"You stupid…You don't know shit. I'm pregnant, you i[...] Doug wants to marry me. It's his child, but I don't want h[...] know. He might make me keep it. I don't want anyone to k[...] have an aunt in Redwood City, not far from Palo Alto. I c[...] with her while I get an abortion. That's why I need your he[...]

"Oh, Jesus, Alexis." He shook his head slowly.

"Yeah, Plato. Yeah." And Alexis cried and moved into[...] He hugged her, trying to remain brotherly. But he felt her[...] chest, and never before had anything felt so good.

"It's okay, Alexis. It's okay," he said, rubbing her ba[ck...] comfort her.

But it wasn't okay. Alexis hugged him tighter, despe[...] through her arms. Plato hadn't had time to think it a[...] he recoiled at the prospect of abortion; he also did[...] of keeping the truth from Doug. He questioned [...] had read many of his namesake's dialogues, so he[...] two about ethics. But he couldn't think straight v[...] him, with her warmth invading his being. He [...] she wasn't thinking straight either. But now [...] make his stand. She held him too tight.

The bus, a Scenic Cruiser, churned northwa[rd...] before it hit San Clemente. Out the windo[w...]

TUKWUT

The sun not fully risen, I'm walking a backcountry trail where unseen eyes bore holes into my neck.

Hunwut, my big Airedale, ranges ahead, zigzagging along game trails, weaving through chaparral, cholla, and scrub oak. Hunwut is a deer dog, trained to walk behind me while hunting, but we're not far from the house so he's running free, having some fun. He's five years old, tough as they come, and mostly conducts himself with aplomb, but in the mornings, he romps like a pup, eyes bright, short tail whipping. He's big for an Airedale, about ninety pounds, bred for size and strength, yet agile and fast, a fullback powering through the line.

But Hunwut isn't all brawn. He's smart too. He cocks his head, watches me, listens when I talk, does what I ask, because, like I say, he's smart. We understand each other. We're roommates. We live in an adobe house that was once my grandparents' on the San Ignacio Indian Reservation in Southern California, about twenty-five miles inland from the Pacific Ocean.

Hunwut is my companion, my coconspirator, my best friend. Now that I'm old, he has my back. He knows who to bark at, who to sidle up to. He never pees or drops a Tootsie Roll in the house. Doesn't chew my shoes or crash through screen doors or claw the leather couch. Never steals food, never gets into the trash, never brings home a dead skunk. He doesn't shed much, doesn't bark needlessly, and doesn't require constant coddling. Oh, he's not perfect. He drinks from the toilet when the mood hits, but I don't care about that. And he snores and farts in his sleep. But then, no doubt, so do I. All in all, he's good company.

Hunwut and I hunt for the freezer. Several times a year we go into the hills above the house to go after a deer. I'm not a trophy hunter. I'm not one of those guys who wants a buck with impressive antlers to hang on the wall. I look for a young spike or forked-horn, tender meat, lighter to carry home. And I'm respectful, always thanking the deer for his sacrifice.

Sure, it would be easier to use a rifle, but I'm old school, so I hunt with a sixty-pound bow, a Fred Bear Kodiak, a short recurve that I can carry without much snagging in the brush. It's not a fancy compound with complicated pulleys and adjustable sights, but bare-bones as it is, it sends an arrow straight and fast.

I don't know how much longer I can shoot the Kodiak. It's getting harder and harder to pull back the string. To keep bow skills sharp you must practice. I have bales of hay out back to practice on, but these days my arms tire before I get many shots in. Yeah, I'm already looking for a lighter bow, but you can't go too light or it won't have stopping power. I don't want to wound deer.

To my bow, I've attached a quiver of sorts that holds four arrows, broadheads with little razor inserts for extra cutting. On my belt, I have a hunting knife that's been sharpened so many times it's ground to the size of a boning knife. It's a stag-handled Camillus that my grandfather gave me when I was twelve. The first thing he did was set me on a bench out back and show me how to sharpen it on a whetstone. "Angle it like this," he said. "It's like trying to cut off a thin slice of stone with each stroke. And that's the way I learned. First the gritty side for proper honing, then the smooth side to polish the edge. "A man keeps his knives sharp," my grandfather said. I've done my best.

Also on my belt, in a leather snap-holster, rides the Colt .45 Model 1911 pistol my grandfather had carried in World War I. Twice the gun saved my grandfather's life in battle. Once, years ago, it had saved mine. It stopped a wild pig that charged me from the brush. The boar's tusks would have ripped me up given the chance. Instead, thanks to the pistol, I made chile verde with the hind quarter. I carry the pistol just in case.

When I hunt, I also carry a light backpack for sundries, like a linen game bag to keep the flies off should I kill a deer, a rope to hang it from a tree limb so I can dress it, a two-liter bottle of water, about a pound of venison jerky for Hunwut and me in case we don't get anything, some kitchen matches—waterproofed by dipping the heads in melted wax and stored in a 20-gauge shotgun shell shoved into a 12-gauge shell—and a few other things.

About twenty-five yards ahead, Hunwut stops at a wide spot in the trail to check on me. He affects a worried look, brows raised with concern. I'm not a fast hill climber anymore. I'm a slow walker. I think Hunwut gets impatient with my pace, but my arthritic knees ache with each step, and it ain't easy to make the climb. Once, I was a fast walker. Back in 1961, the year after I graduated high school, I trapped winters in Idaho. I lived with my dog, another Airedale, named Nanaka, in a log cabin forty-five miles from the nearest town. To get set up, I made two trips to the cabin with a sixty-pound pack on my back to haul supplies. I was a walking fool. I walked my trap line daily, a twelve-mile circuit. Sometimes, when the snow was deep, I checked the traps with snowshoes strapped to my boots. Mostly I trapped coyotes and bobcats. I could get a decent price for hides back then. After two winters, I saved enough to buy a white '57 Chevy pickup with a 327 engine and three on the tree from a Coeur d'Alene Indian guy.

Hunwut yips a couple of times, like he's saying, "Come on, man, get with it. Daylight's burning." Sometimes Hunwut reminds me of John Wayne berating a pilgrim.

The trail isn't steep, but there's definite ascent. An arthritic ligament in my right knee tugs with pain. Nothing to do but walk through it. The doctor at the Indian health clinic recommends a knee replacement, but I'm hoping to avoid that. One thing, I don't have anyone at home to look after me except Hunwut, and I'll be danged if I'm gonna land in some convalescent center, propped in a hospital bed, watching fools yell at each other on *Jerry Springer*.

A roadrunner alights on a head-high boulder to my right. Blurred by my cataracts, he appears almost checkered in blacks and whites. He raises the feather tuft atop his head and gazes at me quizzically. He seems to be chiding, "You should be home, in your recliner, sipping coffee and reading a Tony Hillerman mystery." He's right. But nobody's gonna fill the freezer for me. And I've vowed to live my life the way I've always lived it for as long as I can. I'm not ready for the blanket, dammit.

A red-tailed hawk screeches as several crows dive-bomb him. I think it's a him. Again, my lousy eyesight doesn't allow a clear image. I've admired birds of prey ever since I can remember, red-tailed hawks in particular. I once thought of becoming an ornithologist just to study them. If I have a spirit animal, I guess it would be the red-tail. I've been on vision quests: spent four days in the wild, without food or water, entering the sweat lodge every night, hoping to connect with my spirit animal. I'm no shaman and I wasn't successful, at least I don't think I was. But after my vision quests, when I dream I'm flying, I see the world through the eyes of an airborne red-tailed hawk. So that counts as something, I think. As he passes, I nod in recognition.

We are still climbing, heading toward oak groves that populate hillsides. The sere fall grasses, brittle and wheat-colored, grow where the oak leaves aren't so thick. Each fall I come up here to gather acorns for weewish, a kind of acorn pudding that tastes of my childhood. My grandmother made it all the time. We'd pick enough acorns to last all year. I didn't like it much as a little kid, the flavor too bland, almost muddy. But now I like it with beans, bacon, hot salsa, and a fresh tortilla. I even enjoy it as a breakfast cereal with milk and honey. It's excellent protein, fat free, and doesn't cost anything but the effort to make it. The acorns drop from the oaks in the fall. We're in October now, the acorns almost ready for weewish. I'll be picking soon. The acorns up here grow big and fat, plus I know the best trees. To my left, there's a bedrock mortar, a granite slab the size of a swimming pool with at least a dozen grinding holes filled by dead oak leaves.

I like to imagine ancestor Luiseño women sitting at this milling area, cracking acorns to get the meat inside, grinding it into flour with granite pestles. In the morning, they'd sit in the sun, wearing little more than a skirt of skins, sweat gathering beneath their bare breasts, sometimes singing in chorus, maybe even singing peon songs or bird songs, as they worked. When not singing, they'd talk, laugh, engage in gossip: whose husband was worthless, who was seen sneaking from a kiicha (house) late at night, who couldn't make a decent stew to save her soul. They must have had a different perception of time, absent of pressures, thinking nothing of spending hours grinding acorns, gossiping, and laughing at off-color remarks.

I consider myself a laid-back guy, but I don't have the patience to grind acorns by hand. I bought a small electric mill that in minutes can do what it took the old ones hours to do. So I do make weewish, but I cheat. Not always, but sometimes modernity is a good thing.

Thick oaks grow trailside, trunks rounder than a circus fat lady, bark etched like an old man's wrinkles, branches sprawling to canopy the trail, dawn filtering through leaves to throw a dappled shade.

Morning coolness forms vapor with each exhale. Slanting sunlight elongates shadows, songbirds flit from branch to branch, black beetles lurch along the trail like drunks at closing time, a ground squirrel hightails it into a burrow beneath a stand of paddle cactus. I stop to remove my old army field jacket. I roll it up and stuff it into my pack. The walking has warmed me.

About fifty yards ahead, something is going on. Hunwut barks and then wails. It's a long, forlorn cry, a thing he rarely does unless he hears a siren. I can't see him, he's behind boulders and brush, but I hurry in his direction—something's not right.

As I approach, he's standing, head thrown back in a howl, beside a body half buried by dirt and oak leaves. As I get nearer, I can make out a baby-blue windbreaker, dark-blue running tights, neon-green running shoes, an arm thrown into an impossible angle, a shock of straight black hair, Indian hair. The face is turned away from me. I walk around for a better angle. I see features. I know her. Maria Chaca. She's from here. An ultra-distance runner, an incredible runner who competes in hundred-mile races.

She was probably twenty years old or so, a beautiful girl. A few years back, she was elected Miss Sherman. Thin and lithe and alive, but now her face is contorted in death, her lips colorless, her eyes cold as creek pebbles. She's been disemboweled, her insides eaten out.

I pat Hunwut's head, try to calm him down. "It's okay, boy," I say. But it's not okay. He's upset. I'm upset. A young girl's life has been taken. Some of the blood spilled around her ripped-open torso has dried, so it's not a fresh kill. She probably went for a training run last evening and this happened. I look around for tracks, but too many oak and sycamore leaves blanket the ground. I don't see any tracks.

But I've seen this kind of kill before. I've seen deer with their internal organs removed and then covered with dirt to partially hide the kill for later. I'm pretty sure this is a mountain-lion kill. I look more closely and see the telltale claw marks in the dirt where it scraped the ground to cover the body. *Body*—a cold, uncaring word. It's Maria, dammit. But no, Maria is elsewhere. This is a body, a corpse, organic remains launching toward decay. This body is cat food. I tell myself this to keep emotions at bay.

It seems mountain lions like internal organs best: the heart, liver, kidneys, the lungs. They go for variety meats. The big cats require much meat and will revisit a kill until they've consumed all there is. In a few weeks Maria will be a bone scatter, where even flies won't find much to interest them. I stand for a moment, lift my eyes skyward, and softly sing a death song for the safe passage of her soul.

In the Luiseño tradition, it was believed the soul traveled skyward to become a star. Do I take that literally? Do I believe in the old ways, that the starry heavens are the souls of our ancestors shining down on us? Hell, I don't know. I have no answers about the afterlife. I don't know what happens. I suspect after death our molecules and our life force rejoin the cosmic flow, so the star stories aren't impossible. No matter, I respect life, I respect death, and I pray for Maria. I pray for her parents. I know both. Her mother a Luiseño from here, her father a Hopi, also a long-distance runner. I would often see father and daughter running together in the early mornings on reservation dirt roads, their strides a matching rhythm. If you're a father whose daughter has been killed by a mountain lion, how do you throttle the grief and pain? Do you seek immediate revenge? Does it help to kill the offending mountain lion, give it a taste of its own medicine? Does that make it easier to sleep at night?

Hunwut looks at me, dog eyes full of concern and question, as if asking, "Is there anything we can do?"

All we can do is walk home to call tribal security. Maybe, I consider, it's time to buy a cell phone. I don't really want one, but it would be handy in times like these. Let's hope times like these are extremely—

I sense incoming, then a three-hundred-pound sledgehammer hits me with mortar-fire bombast in the back, pressing me to the ground, forcing all the air from my lungs. Simultaneously, something like knife blades rip and penetrate the back of my neck and head. More knives stab my shoulders, pinning me down; I'm helpless against the strength of it. My nose and mouth smash into the ground. I can't breathe. I gotta lift my head or die. I throw all my strength into arching my back and neck. I manage a quarter inch. I gasp for air. I smell putrid blood and raw meat and evil in the hot breath that bellows about my head. My head and neck are jerked about like a pit bull shaking a chew toy. The imagined knives work themselves deeper into my neck and head. I can hear the bone of my skull splinter under the assault. I want to scream but can't. I hear bestial snorts of effort, or maybe pleasure, but no growls, no roars, no sound other than the lethal dismantling of my body.

The weight, the smell, the strength, the fur, the quickness of it all—my brain registers mountain lion. But I'm surprised how quiet it is. I picture the big cat on my back, clamping its jaws, sinking canines that feel like a saber-toothed tiger's into my neck, controlling me with two-inch claws piercing my shoulders, digging their way into my flesh. But it's so damn quiet. There should at least be a sound track accompanying my death, gourd rattles and bird singers punctuating my demise.

All four years at Sherman Indian High School I wrestled on the school team. Once I wrestled a 300-pound kid totally out of my weight class who was impossible to move. I was 180, but wrestling heavyweight. I was quicker, but then he got the superior position, and it was holy hell to get him off. I could not move him. It was the only time I kneed an opponent in the nuts just to get him off me. I lost both my cool and the match, by disqualification. Sorry, kid, whoever you were. I was wrong for doing it. But here on the trail there are no rules, and I try smashing the cat in the huevos with my right calf. But, once again, I am out of position. I can't generate enough power to do any damage.

Then I hear Hunwut in attack mode, barking and growling. Hunwut must be on the cougar, because it releases its death grip on my neck. The cat rolls off me to get the upper position on Hunwut. I get my first glimpse of the mountain lion, and I'm flabbergasted by its size. It is twice as big as any I've ever seen. A big mountain lion goes maybe 150 pounds. This one surely exceeds 300. It's almost as big as the female African lions I've seen in zoos.

Hunwut is pinned on his back, dwarfed by the huge cat, snapping his jaws to fight back, trying to keep the cat from getting a hold on his throat. But the mountain lion doesn't bother with the throat. He opens his jaws and practically swallows Hunwut's muzzle. Hunwut writhes and struggles but can't get loose. I've never seen Hunwut lose a dogfight. He doesn't start fights, but once in, he fights to win. Hunwut is one big muscle and in terrific shape because we spend most of our time in the hills. But he has no chance. The cat's viselike jaws close on Hunwut's head. Hunwut kicks with all four legs trying to pry the cat off him, but the cat is locked in, the jaws tight, the front claws buried in Hunwut's shoulders. Hunwut fights on, but now he fights in panic. He fights knowing he can't win. His growls turn to whimpers. Hunwut is dying.

I face the fight, so even with my muddy vision I can see the tukwut, the behemoth mountain lion, mauling Hunwut. I want to help him, but dammit, I can't move. I will myself to get up, to do something, anything, but nothing moves. I gasp for air, my stomach muscles involuntarily twitching, the deathmatch of dog and big cat scrambling in the dirt and leaves rages on. Again, I order my body upright, but no dice.

I flex my hands. Will they work? They do. My fingers cooperate. But something is broken. My collarbone grinds with the slightest arm motion. I can't reach my pistol. I must pull it from the holster. I put everything I have into moving my arm down toward it. "Good Christ!" I scream; the pain implodes. I can't let it stop me. I force my way through it. "Sonofabitch," I say. With each move, a red-hot fire poker sticks into my shoulder. The pain isn't as bad when I'm still. I don't wanna move, but I gotta. Sweat and blood drip into my eyes. I inch my hand downward, feeling along my shirt until I touch the oiled leather of the holster flap. "Oh, Christ," I moan, reaching my fingers beneath the flap to unsnap it. The flap lifts, my palm finds the pistol's checkered-walnut grip. l wrap my fingers around the grip. Now, to pull it out. There's no time to do it slowly. Each second, Hunwut gets closer to death. I jerk the pistol up and nearly pass out. Strange psychedelic patterns invade the black tunnels of my vision; my brain whirls.

I extend my arm, the pistol heavy as a sick child, and I rest the butt on the ground to help hold it up. I aim toward the cat and dog fighting in a tumble. If I shoot, I may hit Hunwut. If I don't shoot, he'll die anyway. I yank the trigger. Blam! The second I yanked, I knew it would miss. I aim, no, not aim, point in the general direction of the mountain lion, praying for luck. There is too much motion, too much blurred vision to make out details, but I place the front blade on what I think is the cat's shoulder and squeeze. Blam! I think I hit him but can't be sure. The mountain lion looks at me, mad-dogs me, yellow eyes spewing hate, canines dripping blood. He yearns to kill me. I can tell he burns to rip out my throat. But he isn't a fool. Maybe he's been shot at before. He seems to understand gunfire. He bounds off with a thirty-foot long-jump and slides through the brush too fast for me to get off another shot. For the time being, he figures, escape is the better part of valor.

Hunwut lies on the ground, his front to me. He whines softly, his chest heaving with short, rapid breaths. Hunwut's belly is slit. Blue-gray guts snake from his abdomen into a pile on the ground. I've got to shoot him. He's suffering. I finger the trigger, steadying the pistol best I can. I'm only twenty or so feet away, normally an easy shot. I crook my finger against the cold steel. Blam! But my hand shakes so badly I miss. In the midst of his suffering, Hunwut sends me one final look. A knowing look, a look of acceptance. He's not afraid. I fire again. And again. Each time the pistol biting with recoil. It takes three shots to finally hit him. The .45-caliber lead bullet mushrooms in Hunwut's brain and explodes through. Gray matter and blood splatter out the back. He's dead. My best friend, my companion, my heart, sprawls lifeless, the gunfire still ringing in my ears. Leaves and cat saliva and blood mat his wiry coat. The moment is windless, dead still, not a rustle of oak leaves, even the birds shut up. It's all silence, except for my muffled sob.

The gun falls from my slackened grip. I stay motionless on the ground. I need recovery. I need to take inventory. How bad off am I? Will I die here and now? Rest. Don't think, just concentrate on breath, feel it cool your nasal passages. As long as you're breathing, you aren't dead.

I think of how empty the house will be without Hunwut. I'd planned for us to grow old and die together. No one to talk to over coffee, no one begging for bacon, no one with his head on my lap while I read on the couch. No one.

I think of his puppy days, of him bouncing after a tossed tennis ball, of half-crossed eyes snapping at a moth in the air, the flash of humiliation after tripping over his own feet. Oh, Hunwut, I'm gonna miss the hell out of you.

Fifteen or so minutes pass; I'm still too beat up to move, but I must. I worry the cat will come back to finish me off. Any other mountain lion would be too afraid of humans to come back. But this cat—this cat was different. This cat was malevolent, evil, intent on killing. When I was a boy, my grandfather told me stories about men of power, old Luiseño shamans who could shape-shift, who could transform themselves into bears or other animals of their choosing. I can't help but wonder if this cat isn't one. If not, he's one hell of a freak of nature.

I'm immobilized on the ground but breathing easier. The shock is wearing off, but the pain is coming on. My neck and head feel violated, ventilated. The punctures ache, but it's an extraordinary ache, a deep throbbing, one that directly attacks the nerve endings. My shoulders and back burn even when not moving. Moving them seems out of the question. I have no idea where my bow is, but there's not a chance I could draw back the bowstring even if I knew where it was.

Serrated oak leaves prickle and poke the side of my face. Is it worth the effort to lift my head to relieve the discomfort? Yes, and I try. I do try. But there's just nothing left. I slump-face into the dirt, the weeds, the leaves. The world fades, and I see her. She's wearing her purple-and-gold Sherman Indian High School volleyball uniform, satin shorts and tank top; long, black hair cascading to the waistband of her shorts. She's not tall and leggy but short and compact, more quarter horse than thoroughbred. One look and my heart flip-flops. We were both freshmen, both away from home for the first time, but she farther away from home than I. It took a while to get to know her. She was from the Coeur d'Alene rez in Idaho, an out-of-state Indian, so in the beginning, we had no friends in common. But over time, in the Sherman dining hall, I would take my tray a little closer to her, eat my stewed tomatoes and biscuits, my hamburger patty, my green salad topped with Thousand Island dressing, my raspberry Jell-O, my glass of milk, and watch her furtively.

Her face was absent of sharp angles, not chubby, but rounded, her cheeks and chin softened by curves, her nose part of her symmetry and grace. She didn't just smile with her mouth, her whole being smiled, her eyes beaming with all that was good in the world. She liked to laugh, but not loud and boisterous like most high school girls craving attention. She laughed because she was amused, entertained, joyful of the moment. I loved her before she said one word to me.

At a school dance in the gym still smelling of basketball sweat, Tommy Nez played records through the school's big Voice of the Theater speakers, and we, Maeva and I, ended up being partners in the Stroll. As the Diamonds sang, we navigated through the corridor of students, girls on one side, guys opposite, she actually dancing, me doing my best. She wore a knee-length, blue-plaid skirt and a denim shirt with two-toned cowboy boots. A beaded choker with an abalone centerpiece graced her neck. She smiled like a beatitude as she danced, did a little shimmy as the saxophones bawled, and was smooth enough to incorporate a spin into the step that was way beyond my dancing skills.

The song ended, our dance ended, but I didn't want our time to end.

"Care for a Coke?" I asked.

"No thanks," she said, her eyes talking mischief.

My heart sank, me thinking she didn't like me, then she smiled. "But I'll take a Pepsi."

We walked to the refreshment table and I bought us both Pepsis. Cans of Pepsi were stored on ice in galvanized tubs. A teacher punched holes in the cans with a church key and took my two quarters.

"Come on," I said.

Another song came on, this one a grinder. I considered whisking her out to the dance floor, a chance to rub up against her. Instead, I said, "Outside?" and we left the gym and sat on a bench in the breezeway. Sure I wanted to feel her, but I wanted to know her.

It was October, the first dance of the year, and it was still warm in Riverside, an Indian-summer breeze rattling the many palms that towered on the campus.

She sat, sipped her Pepsi, and asked me, "So why are you always looking at me?"

"I'm not…," I said.

"You're not? You are."

"You're crazy," I said.

"Nope, I think you like me. I think I know when a boy likes me, and you like me."

I tried to change the subject. "So what's your name?"

"You know my name. Why are you playing?"

This girl. Young, a freshman, but man, bold.

"I like you, Manny Sobenish. You see, I know your name. And I'm not playing."

The breeze shifted a lock of hair over her eye and she reached over to tuck it behind her ear. She looked at me half serious, half smiling. She knew what she was up to. She was butter to my cornbread.

"Okay, shoot me. I do like you. No, I take that back. Maybe I was born for you," I said.

A stinging pain between my right thumb and forefinger brings me to consciousness. A red ant sinks its jibs into my flesh, injecting formic acid. I swipe the ant off in the dirt. Which hurts worse: the ant bite or my shoulders? It's a toss-up. Red ants mill in and out of a mound about three feet from where I lie. I need to move.

I realize I had passed out. I don't know for how long, but the sun is higher now, edging toward midmorning. Maybe I had been unconscious a couple of hours. I am beyond stiff but must marshal my will. I strain to grab the pistol by its grip. I pull my arms beneath me and seek to crawl away. Something is wrong with my legs. Could the cougar landing on my back have broken it? I can't move my legs. I can barely feel them. But I can feel wetness at my groin. I've pissed my pants. I should be embarrassed, but it's the least of my worries.

I catch sight of Hunwut, which rekindles my loss. Some hundred feet away, various bacteria and insects work on Maria's corpse, digesting it, returning it to the universe. This plot of earth beneath the sacred oaks is becoming quite the killing field. I inch myself away, dragging through the detritus of leaves, weeds, and dirt. Each inch of travel requires maximum effort, like I'm in the weight room deadlifting five hundred pounds. I break into a sweat, my muscles shaking. After twenty minutes, I go maybe five feet. I'm all in, can't go farther. But at least I've found a patch of bare ground, not so many leaves to prick my skin, no ants that I can see. I lay my cheek in the dirt.

Finally, after more than two years of nocturnal emissions, of feverish make-out sessions that always ended in "Stop, enough," of cold showers and blue balls, we made love. Earlier that Friday, I hung out in front of a Chinese-owned liquor store and paid a wino a few bucks to buy me a couple of bottles of Ripple. l bribed my roommate to crash in another room, and Maeva came over. She was sweet sixteen, the sexual longing no easier on her. She arrived a virgin but knew she'd leave a woman. I was a virgin too, but raw desire overpowered fears.

I had a record player, a school gift from my Aunt Vivian. Maeva liked country; I liked blues and Motown—I had a stack of both. I had put mattresses on the floor, covered them with sheets and blankets, plenty of room to roll, the way Etta James intended it.

She knocked at the door, a gentle fingernail tapping, like a secret exchange. I opened it. She stood in the doorway, in her favorite jeans and a T-shirt, in beauty. Some asshole down the hall howled like a coyote. She stepped in unashamed. I closed the door. Shut off the light. Made the world go away.

"Hi," she said.

"Hello," I replied.

Both of us a little off balance, both of us managing the moment with false bravado. I opened the wine and poured us each a glass. She took a chair, my roommate Biggy's desk chair. I pulled out mine to face her. I handed her the glass of wine, a juice glass I had pilfered from the cafeteria. She sipped, made a face. I sipped.

"The first is always the roughest," I said.

"So they say," she said with wider meaning.

I put on Hank Williams. We drank wine, talked of horses, of that afternoon's wrestling match, of college dreams, of the girl who had head lice, all the while searching each other's eyes for signs of doubt. I had no doubt. I knew, even then, she was the one. I sensed she felt the same. Virginity be damned—we craved touch.

We stood to slow dance, Hank Williams singing "I'm So Lonesome I Could Cry." She sighed and pushed me back from her. I lifted her T-shirt over her head and tossed it. She wasn't wearing a bra. I unsnapped her jeans, unzipped them, worked them down to her ankles. She wore white silk panties. She kicked off her flip-flops and removed her jeans. She unbuttoned my shirt. Undid my jeans. And we embraced for the first time with no clothes between us, no fabric blocking the warm velvet of her skin against mine.

We kissed, lowering in unison onto the makeshift bed. She turned away from me, to remove her panties. She knelt with her back to me. In the moonlight, I studied the brown loveliness of her back, moon-shadows defining her shoulder blades, the slink of her spine, the two dimples in the small of her back. I traced my fingertips along her vertebrae, circling the dimples. She shivered with gooseflesh, turned toward me, her nipples erect.

A blue-bellied lizard cranes his prehistoric eye toward mine. He does push-ups, his tapered tail moving to and fro. He's inches from my face, almost too close for me to focus. He scurries away. Why? I hadn't moved, except to open my eyes. Maybe he senses my consciousness and flees possible danger. I'm fond of lizards, I wouldn't hurt him, but he doesn't know that. Overhead, a red-tailed hawk screeches.

Then I hear the ever-so-gentle crunch of dead leaves. My stomach lurches. Fear rises like bile in my throat. I grab hold of the pistol. The sound comes from behind me. I can't see behind me. Sometimes I think it's a human disadvantage that our eyes face forward, limiting our range of vision. I gotta think it's easier for the lizard with the eyes on the sides of his head to see behind him.

I still have my backpack on, which further blocks my view, but I rotate a few degrees so I can see at least a little behind me. My grip tightens on the Colt. I scan the terrain. Oak trees with spreading branches throwing shadows, granite boulders big as Volkswagens, paddle and cholla cactus growing where the rocks allow, sugar-bush and scrub oak, white sage, chaparral. I don't see any hulking movement. But I sense something. My radar detects a presence; even though I can't see it, it's here. I can almost smell the bad heading my way.

There. More crackling leaves, nature's warning system. Something's afoot and getting closer. Now what? I'm seventy-four years old. Even at my best, I'm hardly fast and mobile anymore. Now I'm all chewed up and the pain is debilitating. I'd best play dead. I can't move, better to not even try. Movement attracts house cats, and I doubt cougars are any different. Just be still. I don't have much choice.

The Colt carries seven rounds in the clip; there's two left. I have another clip in the backpack, but given the state of my shoulders, I doubt I can get the backpack off to open it. Not without massive pain and the attention that would attract. There's absolutely no chance of reaching around to open it. My shoulders are so tight with age and arthritis, I couldn't do it even if I wasn't all torn up.

More leaves crackle. Even closer. I close my eyes, try to see through my ears, intent on every sound. The big cat feels his way toward me, many seconds between each step, padding for quiet, but the dead leaves betray him. I hear his breathing. I smell his musky stench. Christ, should I just try opening fire? Maybe it would scare him off. But with only two shots left, I can't waste any. I need a killing shot. If I just wound him and he comes at me, I become Purina cat chow. I hear him, so close. I hear his breathing, deep and rattling. He's over me. He's sniffing my ear, his whiskers brushing my earlobe. I can't turn fast enough to get a shot off before he'd swipe me with those claws. I remember how lightning fast he is, I remember his unconquerable strength. "It's a good day to die," Indians say in movies. But is it? It doesn't feel that way to me. I'd pictured a more dignified ending for me. I'm okay with death—in fact, many times I've yearned for it. But I don't want to end up as cat food. Not my idea of a poetic way out. My grandfather took his last breath in his bed, died in his sleep at the age of eighty-nine, two days before his ninetieth birthday. That's the way to go. I hope to go similarly. With a scrap of dignity, in my sleep, before I get too old to take care of myself—in the same bed he died in.

His paw is right by my face. It's massive. Tawny brown, tufts of white fur on the back side. He's in stalk mode, so the claws are retracted. A couple more steps and I might have a forward shot at him. But he has to be in front for me to shoot. I can't move fast enough to get off a shot directly above me, or even to the side of me. Maybe he's going to pass me by to feed on Maria. Jesus, how can I just lie here while he's gnawing on her bones? I would hear the bones crack from here. I remember her at the store, at the post office, at funerals, always polite, courteous, full of life. Never flashed a gang sign or raised hell, at least not that I ever saw. She was a sweet kid, a girl who could run forever. Now she will never get to realize her potential. Why do bad things happen to good people?

Without warning the big cat swipes me with his right paw, slamming my right armpit, flipping me over onto my back. Like a cat toying with a catnip mouse, he tears at me again, this time with his left paw, gashing my right cheek. He's too fast, too strong for me to play it cool. He's on me, his mouth gaping, his teeth yellowed but shiny with saliva. His breath a blast furnace of carnivorous funk. He looks me in the eye. His yellow eyes are demonic and knowing. I raise the pistol and pull the trigger, hoping to hit him in the throat. He's moving, moving too fast to hit him clean, but I think the bullet grazes his neck. I fire again, aiming for his torso, hoping for his heart, but it's all happening in such a blur I don't know what I hit. But I hit something. He leaps, twisting, like a fish trying to throw the hook, gyrating midair, fighting to right his body to land on his feet. But he doesn't. He lands with an air-crushing thud on his side.

For the first time, I hear him snarl. My stomach twists at the menace of the growl. Is he gathering himself to come at me again? I aim my gun at him. He's hurt. He's on the ground scrambling to get upright. The blade of the front sight is lined up with his chest. I pull the trigger, but the pistol dry fires. The gun is empty. I can't get the other clip from my backpack. My arms won't bend enough for me to loosen the pack.

With my right hand, I replace the pistol in its holster. With my left, I find my knife and pull it from the sheath. Tukwut is up now. Pissed off, but unsteady, he steals off, into the brush. I can't see him, but I gotta think he's still there, licking his wounds, watching. He'll be back. I have no doubt. I saw it in his eyes. He intends to kill me.

I'm so thirsty. There's an out-of-reach water bottle in the backpack. But wait. I have the knife—why not cut the straps? Maybe I can move my arm over enough to saw the knife blade through the straps. My knife, razor sharp, makes easy work of the nylon strap. I switch hands and cut the other strap. I'm free from the back. I roll, but like a fool I roll the wrong way. I can't reach back to unzip the pack. I have to roll the other way. I re-sheathe the knife, slide my elbow beneath me, and rock my body. Without use of my legs, I have no purchase to push myself over. "God almighty," I blurt. Pain rockets through me. But a half-dozen rocking motions get me on my side facing the pack. I unzip it and find the water bottle. It's a two-liter plastic bottle that once held seltzer water. I carry that much water, enough for Hunwut and me. The thought of Hunwut makes me sob. I feel stupid, ashamed, but can't stop the tears. I'm a seventy-four-year-old man weeping in the dirt. Soon I realize I'm not weeping just for Hunwut, I'm weeping for me, for my misspent life, for Maeva.

It's not the first time. Old age is crying time. The tears come much too easily now that I'm old. I blame biology, the inevitable loss of testosterone with time, but there is also the inherent sadness that accompanies Indian life, the loss of all the people you have known and cared about now gone, the finality of death, the impending absence of you. All this builds, all coming at you at once, and you collapse into tears. I'm the sad man.

With shaky hands, I untwist the plastic cap, but not all the way. I can't lift the bottle to my mouth. So I lay it on its side and scoot it toward my mouth. I remove the cap and fit my mouth around the opening. The water isn't cold, but it's wet. I swallow, keep swallowing all I can. I'm beyond dehydrated. To help the flow, with supreme effort I lift the bottle an inch or so with my left hand. I drink till I can't anymore and then replace the cap.

I feel around my pack for the extra clip. I drop the empty clip from my pistol, slide in the full one. I put the water back into the pack. Dragging my pack, I crawl, inch by inch, to the base of a gnarled oak tree. I look up the trunk and spot the place where woodpeckers have bored holes into the bark and stuffed in acorns for winter storage. I set the pack against the tree, to use as a backrest. It's getting cold; I pull out my jacket. No way I can put it on, but maybe I can use it as a blanket. One last push, to rest against the pack, rest against the tree. I won't have to worry so much about the cat coming up behind me. I've got a full clip, I still have my knife, here I'll make my stand. Okay, cat, let's do this.

Dusk lowers the blinds on Mother Earth. Somewhere behind me, somewhere I can't much see, Grandfather Sun paints the skyline pink. It's a slow advance of darkness, almost imperceptible. And I think this is nature's way, the slow flow of all things. Nothing is permanent. Everything is imperceptible change. Even I, I am not constant, my molecules release into the atmosphere, new cells replace dead cells; over time I will simply be a version of my old self. Nothing is fixed. Nothing is permanent. Not even permanence is permanent. I chuckle to myself. Am I losing it?

I am positioned against my pack, supported by the oak, the pistol in my lap, the birds winging toward night roosts, the crickets tuning up their instruments, the air still; even the leaves stop talking. I've been hurting so long, in so much pain, I'm almost numb to it. It's like when you get so wet you can't get any wetter.

I close my eyes to listen deeply, focusing to hear it all, not just the notes but the space between the notes too. I hear the birds settling in, fluffing their feathers, twittering their evening song. In the distance I hear civilization, a jet airliner slicing through the sky, ferrying passengers to air-conditioned airports, maybe to a Styrofoam teriyaki bowl at the food court. I hear my blood pumping, I hear my breath, I hear my existence. I hear the universe's—one song.

Maeva and I two-stepped to a cover band's version of "San Antonio Rose." It wasn't great music, but it was music. I had borrowed a friend's car to drive us on a Saturday night to Los Tules, a dance held in a Quonset hut where Indians gathered. It was kind of far from Sherman, but I wanted her to mix with rez locals, for her to get a feel for California Indian life.

"Deep within my heart lies a melody…" She knew every verse and sang the words in my ear as we danced, her breath, warm and damp, sending promises down my spine. Cowboy hats, many with a feather jammed into the band, drifted around the floor as couples twirled. It was jacket weather, but a venerable wood stove fought back the cold. Also, to fight back the cold, I had two pints of Four Roses bourbon, one for each pocket of my peacoat. Between songs we'd drift over to the coat to sneak drinks. Maeva had warmed to the whiskey and stopped making faces with each swallow.

"Not so bad now, is it?" I said.

"Shut up," she said.

"What?"

"Stop making fun of me," she said.

I kissed her and tasted the sting of whiskey on her lips.

"No, I would never do that," I said.

"Yeah, right." We both laughed.

"Wanna go outside?"

"Sure," she said.

Men and women in cowboy hats stood around an oak fire, flames yellow and blue dancing skyward. A small wind blew from the west, just enough to blow the smoke in one direction. I recognized a few folks I knew from Rincon, some from Pechanga, but didn't go out of my way to introduce. Call me selfish, but I wanted Maeva to myself.

We warmed by the fire, taking slugs of whiskey, glowing with fire and strong drink. I slipped my arm around her waist.

"I love you, girl," I said.

"What?"

She'd heard me, she just wanted to hear me say it again.

"I said, 'I love you.'" I had no second thoughts about saying it. No thoughts of entrapment, no fear of commitment, no worries about our future together.

"I know," she said. "I can feel it. And that makes me happy. How awful to love you, and for you not to love me back."

"So you love me?"

"Course I do. I'm sure you know I do. I'm yours. I'll always be yours."

"Let's drink to forever," I said.

I held the bottle of Four Roses up to the fire, yellow fire glow glinting in amber bourbon.

"Forever," I said, and drank.

"Forever," she said, and drank. I looked at her, she smiled at me, her eyes a gathering of heavenly delights. And I felt a crescendo, as close as a human can get to ecstasy.

We danced and drank and laughed and sang. The music ended, the band packed their instruments, and we stumbled into the night out to the car—a Plymouth Fury, owned by Dusty, an Oklahoma Cherokee classmate, who'd bought the car with oil-lease money.

We played the radio. Chuck Berry singing "Johnny B. Goode," and we sang along, reveling in our youth, rocking to the beat, her face bathed in green dashboard light.

Sherman curfew was midnight, it was already 2:00 a.m., but neither of us cared. On some nights time means nothing. We were too full of life, too full of love, too wrapped up in each other to give a shit. We were on a straightaway, climbing a hill. Up ahead, I saw the headlights, but no warning registered in my brain. But as they came closer, they jarred me to awareness. They were too damn close. They aimed right at us. I pulled the Fury's steering wheel to miss them, skidding onto the shoulder. The cattle truck did miss us, but we clipped a boulder, which spun us across the road over the edge of an embankment. When I came to, Maeva's head and shoulders had thrust through the windshield. She was imprisoned in shattered glass. The steering wheel had saved me.

I'll never know. If sober, could I have avoided that truck? Could I have hit the shoulder, stayed on the road, and prevented Maeva's death? I'll never know.

Time may at times feel meaningless, but finality is real. I know finality. I know the end. After that night, I never drank again. I never held another woman. I breathed, but never truly lived. Maeva died that night. So did most of me. Some wrongs can't be redeemed. For more than sixty years I've sought redemption, but there's no such thing. You say you forgive yourself, but it just doesn't wash. I have scars of self-immolation, nights with an X-Acto knife when I'd sliced through my flesh with thoughts of bleeding the life out of me. There is no escape, no relief from self-hate, no solace save death.

The lion is back. It's dark. I can't see him, I can't hear him, but I sense him. Stars wink in the indigo sky. Are you my relatives? Gramps, are you up there watching? Dad. I didn't know you. You died in the Bataan Death March. Are you watching me, Mom? I didn't know you, but I did suckle at your breast. You cooed at me, made me smile. You found death in a bottle of sleeping pills. Maybe your suicide saved me from my own. Star brights, do you see me? Your son, Manuel. I'm here. Maeva, my love, I'm here, longing.

I see the yellow eyes first, about fifty feet away, the eerie radiation of feline night vision. It doesn't have to be this way. You can just walk away. Find yourself a mate on yonder mountain. But maybe you aren't animal. Maybe you are possessed. Maybe this is fate.

I get the pistol ready. Let's do this, you fucker. You killed Maria, and you wanna kill me. But I'm not that easy to kill. Like the song says, "Come and get your love." I have a full clip of .45s in my lap. I chamber a round. I think of Maeva's tweed suitcase of 45s—country and rockabilly. She'd play them in stacks and tell stories about barrel racing her Appaloosa filly at the county fair.

He advances. But slowly. One careful step at a time, the eyes getting closer, bigger, more hateful. Under different circumstances, I would have considered him beautiful, so big, so felinely muscled, so physically in control. He is at least thirty feet away, but even with his own bullet pain, he moves with deliberation. He crouches, pulling his rear legs under him. Then he springs, three hundred pounds of him, claws extended, fangs bared, aimed at my face. Airborne, he flies straight at me. No snarl. No growl. Silent death. I lift the pistol. I don't think; I act in reflex. Pull the trigger, pull the trigger, pull it again. Blam, blam, blam. I hit him, I know I hit him. I know it. But he keeps coming. I empty the gun into him. I can hear slugs slamming into his flesh, see him jerk midair as the bullets penetrate, then expand to rip his flesh. He takes all seven rounds at point-blank range. He takes them; he keeps flying toward me.

Sherman Indian High School has a cemetery where indigent Indian kids who die while attending school get buried. There was talk of burying her there. But I loaded her casket into my grandfather's old Chevy pickup and drove it to the Coeur d'Alene Reservation of open fields surrounded by piney forests. I got directions to her parents' house from an outlying trading post. The woman behind the counter, her braids wrapped in rabbit skin, had heard about Maeva's death. She wrinkled her nose at me like I was Limburger cheese. Maeva's was a small white house with a green door. I knocked at the door. Her father opened it. He took one look, balled his fist, and socked me. Socked me hard. He socked me again, his knuckles against my jaw, and I went down. Crazed by grief, he kicked the shit out of me. I let him. Him crying, cursing the gods. Me crying, cursing myself. His wife, Maeva's mother, stopped him from killing me. I wouldn't have cared if he did.

Tukwut is a projectile in slow motion. His long body extended, ears flat. He tears into me, tooth and claw shredding my flesh; he snorts with exertion. The back of my head bounces off the oak trunk, he clamps his jaws over my face, his teeth embedding into my cheeks, his claws ripping my chest. I am locked in his embrace. By reflex, I bend my chin to my chest, trying to protect my neck. I don't want him ripping my jugular. I fumble around my belt and locate my knife. I pull the knife and plunge the blade into his underbelly. I pull it out to stab him again, but he backs off and swats the knife out of my hand. It goes flying; I hear it clink against a rock in the distance.

He tackles me again, again going for my face. I have no weapon, but like a boxer I hold up my arms to protect my face. Like a boxer, he knocks away my arms, lunging again for my face. But he's noticeably weaker; he doesn't have the same strength, the same force. He's like a wrestling opponent who's running out of gas. He's got slugs in him, maybe even seven of them. Finally, maybe they are doing their work. God, please stop him. Hard to break the mission habit.

He's dying, his weight collapsing on my lap. He's panting, heaving because he can't get enough oxygen. Blood seeps from his mouth, pours out between his teeth, down his rough tongue, and soaks into my jeans. He's a big house cat, asking to be petted. And then he's no more. He's dead, his eyes empty, lifeless, staring into nothingness.

I can't move. I have no wish to move. I'm drifting off. In my dream, I hear voices.

"Over here," someone shouts.

"Holy Christ," another says.

I glimpse two men in tribal ranger uniforms. They must be searching for Maria.

I'm leaving my body. I hover about ten feet above the scene. I see the tribal rangers, I see Maria, I see Hunwut. I see me, bloodied against the oak, Tukwut in my lap. I don't know if I see myself, with my eyes, or if it's just the concept of me on the ground I see. But for a moment, I feel peace. For the first time since the wreck, there is no internal gnashing over what I have done. Who knows, maybe I will see Maeva, get to tell her I'm sorry.

And soon there is nothing. Sweet oblivion.

BIRD SONGS DON'T LIE

A bird-song night winds down, the singers have flown, the fire sputters in embers. A fifth of peppermint schnapps makes the rounds. Franklin—he insists on being called Franklin, not Frank, not Frankie, but Franklin—lifts the bottle to his lips, tilts, and swallows. Franklin's braid reaches his belt, his loose-fitting ribbon shirt is red with black ribbons, a rolled red bandana wraps his head. He's convinced chicks dig red.

He's laying it on thick: "I've got maybe a hundred or so head grazing the rez. Prolly, take us a couple weeks to pop them out of the brush," he says, like he's effing John Wayne.

Such bullshit. In reality, he's got two young steers in a pen out back of his house. When he forgets, which is often, his gram has to pitch them alfalfa else they starve. When it comes to animal husbandry, Franklin is piss poor. But he's my best friend; I can't call out his bullshit.

He hands her the bottle. She's a peach from Peach Springs, hint of baby fat rounding out baby-maker hips, feline eyes daring you to love her, her smile a blend of brazen and coy. She dances the birds. Me and Franklin sing the birds. I couldn't help but notice her in the lineup of dancers, wish for her, lust after her. Movements so smooth, so seamless, her storyteller hands embellishing, her long red skirt a swirl, its hem brushing doeskin moccasins. Her silk blouse, a lighter rose, does little to conceal her curves, and neither do the strands of seashell beads draping her neck. She wears no lipstick, no other makeup except reddish eye shadow.

No dainty swig for her. She pulls at the bottle, her throat in peristaltic motion, like a snake swallowing a mouse. I admire her enthusiasm.

Earlier, during a break in the bird singing, while in line at the frybread stand, it slips out. I try to silence it, but it rips like a sheet.

"Leh," she says, from in front of me. "Might wanna check your shorts." She giggles—creek water chuckling over pebbles.

"Jesus," I say, wishing she hadn't heard. "Excuse me."

"No matter. No harm done."

"My mamma taught me to say 'excuse me.' I'm Larry, by the way, but people call me Bird. No basketball cracks, please."

No hint that she gets what I mean. I doubt she knows who Larry Bird is.

"Do I really want to know you, Bird—a farter?" She giggles again. "I'm Priscilla, but people call me Sister. No Elvis cracks, please."

"Sister?"

"Yeah, it's a dad thing."

She orders an Indian taco with extra cheese from a gray-haired grandmother in a housedress behind the counter. Another woman in running shoes tends to frybread bubbling in oil.

"And a Pepsi," she says to the counter woman.

"Pepsi. The Indian Killer?" I say, teasingly.

She turns to face me. Her plucked eyebrows arch with false menace. "So what are you, the sugar police? Besides, it's my birthday;

I'm having a Pepsi. Got a problem? Don't you ever celebrate? No, you're probably Mr. Perfect."

"Geez, sorry. Didn't mean to…"

"Sure you did. You think you're smarter than me. I see superiority written all over your big face."

I can tell she's just raising hell. She can't hide her smile.

"Sorry. Guess I'm a pig for being concerned for your health. But hey: Happy birthday, beautiful."

"Mmmm, nice recovery, Bird," she says, flipping the hair out of her eyes.

"How about letting me pay for your Indian taco?" I say. "A little birthday gesture?"

"Naw, keep your per cap. I'll pay for my own."

I shrug. "Just tryin'…"

"I know what you're tryin'…"

She turns back to the counter, where her order steams: golden frybread topped with fresh boiled beans, shredded beef, lettuce, tomato, and yellow cheese. The counter woman pulls a Pepsi from the ice, the can dripping with condensation. Been a long time since I've had a Pepsi. It tempts mightily.

Sister reaches into her blouse to retrieve a sweaty twenty-dollar bill from her bra, hands it over. I didn't know girls still carried money in their bras. My grandmother used to, but I hadn't seen it done in years. I guess when you ain't got pockets…

Sister accepts her change, drops money into the tip jar, reinserts folded bills in her bra. As she leans forward, I glimpse an inviting divide. She grabs a plastic squirt bottle to drown her taco in hot sauce. I'm transfixed. I watch her long hair, a little damp with sweat, embrace her face. The squirt bottle makes a farting sound as she squeezes. We both laugh.

"That wasn't me," she says.

"Yeah, right."

We laugh again. Laughter comes easy to us.

The woman behind the counter, perspiration dappling her upper lip, clears her throat impatiently for my order. I ask for an Indian taco and a Pepsi. Sister wheels when she hears "Pepsi," then snickers, eyes mocking.

"What the hell. If you can have one, so can I," I say.

Frenzied winged insects clink against the light bulb burning overhead. Sizzling frybread sings its own song. A long-handled fork clanks against cast iron as running-shoes woman flips frybread browning in hot fat.

"Listen, we got off to a bad start," I say.

"Yep, kind of a stinky start." She smiles.

"Let's be friends. Where're you from?"

"Peach Springs."

"Okay, I know it, we've sung there. Cool place."

"Then maybe I've seen you before. Where're you from?"

"I'm from here. San Ignacio, born and bred."

"So are the stories true?"

"What stories?"

"That you guys still boil dogs for stew?"

I'm dumbstruck. But I guess my face tells the story.

"Take it easy, Tonto. I'm just shittin' you."

My Indian taco is ready. She waits while I squirt on hot sauce and get my Pepsi.

"Come on," she says.

I follow her to a couple of hay bales between ramadas, where we sit.

"Here," she says, handing me a napkin, eye-rolling like a mother to a dreamy child. I'd forgotten to get one. My gourd rattle (it was once my grandfather's, painted blue-black with lightning streaks) hangs from a leather thong around my wrist. I slip it off, set it next to me.

I open the Pepsi, the fizz erupts, and I drink deep. The sweet burn feels alive, the carbonation soothing my song-roughened pipes.

"Good call," I say.

She questions with a look.

"The Pepsi."

"Stick with me, grasshopper," she says. The girl has attitude that unsettles. She's a handful.

In the distance, a rez dog dashes in, full lope, from the fiesta grounds toward the brushy perimeter.

"Look," she says, pointing. "Poor thing's scared of ending up in a San Iggy stewpot."

"Again with the dogs?"

"All right, I'll stop." But then she curls her tongue and whistles like a puppy squealing after being hit by a car. She imitates masterfully. Some people even turn to look.

"Knock it off," I say.

She shows her Pepsodent smile. We're sitting in shadows, but her teeth glow like a luminous clock. I study the contours of her face. It's a face without corners, smooth, soft, comforting—combination of schoolgirl and matriarch.

She really is a beauty. Bangs sweep over her left eye. She flicks them into place with a shake of her head. I'm in lust. I've been in lust before, but not like this. It's like she has my heart cupped in her hands, controlling its beat.

The conversation lulls. Maybe I can make her laugh.

"So where have you been all my life?" I say.

"If you're gonna get all corny, at least make it fresh corn."

"Just joking."

"Pretty sad attempt, but points for trying."

"Aha! Is she beginning to like me?" I say aloud to nobody.

She smiles, then bites into her Indian taco, toppings threatening to spill over. I hand her my napkin.

*B*ack at the fire, it's almost 2:00 a.m.; a silver moon hangs like a scimitar. Somewhere in the nearby foothills, coyotes yowl in a minor key; Sister hands me the schnapps and I drink, but not much. I don't drink much. I've seen too much bad drinking in my life.

She stands between Franklin and I, her traditional attire reflecting reds from the dying fire, her eyes bright with mischief. We three are the last at the fire. Around us, ramadas darken as they close, cars crawl out of the parking lot. Overhead, several small bats flap herky-jerky in the night sky.

Franklin is telling her how he's going to UC Berkeley in the fall. He's gonna major in American Indian studies, then go on to law school. Gonna to be a warrior for the people in the courts. Total bullshit. He works as a parking valet at Two Suns Casino. He's not going to Berkeley. Hell, he barely graduated high school. He might not have graduated if I hadn't let him copy my homework all through school.

"Really? Berkeley? Very cool. That's a hard school to get into. You must be smart," Sister says. She nips from the schnapps bottle.

"Finally, someone who gets me," Franklin says.

He's unabashed. He knows I know he's lying to impress this girl but doesn't care. He scents prey.

"So, who's gonna take care of all your cattle while you're at school?" she asks, a hit of snark in her tone.

Franklin marches on. "Good thing about cattle is they pretty much take care of themselves. And I'll be home now and then to look after them, you know, roundup and brand on spring break," he says, taking a shot from the bottle she passes to him. I got to hand it to him, he's handling.

"And you?" I ask Sister. "You going to college in the fall?"

"Not this fall, maybe next," she says. "I still have to graduate from high school."

Uh-oh. Jailbait. She looks older, but she's probably only sixteen or seventeen. She's a babe in the woods.

Undeterred, Franklin presses on. "No way. You're way too fine to be in high school. What are you, head cheerleader?"

Sister appears to buy this line. Is he getting to her, infiltrating her defenses? Please don't get sucked in. Come on, Sister, don't be dumb.

"Today is Sister's birthday," I say. "Here's to how old? Seventeen?" I guess, raising the bottle in a toast.

"Yep, seventeen," she says. "Seventeen going on twenty-seven." She tips the schnapps, feigning bravado.

"Whoo, a birthday girl," Franklin says. "Well, happy birthday, Sister." Then, with a hint of snake oil, he adds, "Maybe later I can give you a little present."

"Yeah? How little?" Sister says. I snort Schnapps in laughter.

With the confidence of a swordsman, Franklin replies, "Not so little."

Balls to the wall, Franklin, alpha rez dog, is going for it. I'm quickly feeling the outsider to their give and take. Ain't I the one who brought her to the fire? But his bullshit is outmaneuvering me. Should I step up my game? But she's only seventeen. But she's hot. But she's only seventeen. But I felt something between us. But she's jailbait. She wouldn't be the first seventeen-year-old to…But I'm at Stanford in a month. Besides, she lives too far. How could things work? I think too much. Be like Franklin. He doesn't think. He just does. It's why he snags ten to your one. No, just no. Sometimes inaction is the best action, I try to convince myself.

The fire is next to dead. The air chills. Sister's silk blouse is too thin for warmth; goose bumps ripple her arms. Franklin puts an arm around her, his fingers on her flesh. Envy pangs me. He points to the few cars parked about seventy-five yards away.

"You see that van? That's my van. It's warm in there. I've got music. I've got herb. I have another bottle of schnapps. I'm inviting you out of the cold."

Sister looks at him. Then at me. I give her an "it's up to you" shrug.

Franklin and I grew up together: We played catch with a baseball wrapped in electrical tape. We fought with swords made from fence pickets, using garbage-can lids for shields. We threw darts fashioned from corncobs and turkey feathers. I still have a scar where a nail-tipped dart stuck in my thigh. We've had each other's backs all these years.

He's saved my bacon several times. Once, when we played football in Bloomington, some gang guys confronted us after the game, a game we won. One pimple-faced guy came at me with a shank. Franklin palmed a rock and with no hesitation swung a roundhouse right, thwacking the side of the guy's head. The dude crumpled like an empty suit. Laid him out flat. And that's why they say bros before hoes.

His arm snakes around her shoulders, guiding her to the van. I stay where I am. I try to get all sour grapes about it. She went with him too easy; she ain't worth bothering with. But her smile. Her smile kills me. In her eyes I see my heart. Franklin will play hide the sausage, zip up, and forget her. But she and I, we could have been something. Something outstanding. But isn't that always the way. Your next love is going to be your best love. But then a Franklin comes along. I'm so tired of thinking.

How long am going to stay at this dying fire? I could just walk home, but I feel something's left undone.

As I stand, the night surrounds me. I conjure childhood memories of grizzled old guys in black vests, white T-shirts, beat-up cowboy hats hanging at the old man's bench, swilling Thunderbird, singing birds on drunken nights. It was all impromptu, spontaneous, singing for the hell of it, for the love of it. They rattle with PET milk cans or beer cans with pebbles inside, sticks stuck into holes for handles. They sing in unison, their Bull Durham voices aimed skyward, the wine and the songs transporting them to youth, back to when they sang with their own grandfathers. They sang, consumed by song, wine-soaked, tearful, sometimes snot dripping from their noses. They sang, and rattled, and grunted. They did it because they had no choice, the way water must run downhill.

My rattle still hangs from my wrist. One song to end the night? Why not? A nightcap of sorts. I grip the cottonwood handle smoothed fifty years before by my grandfather's pocketknife. We had the same hands. The handle feels custom-fitted to mine. I shake the rattle in familiar long-short rhythms, the soft explosion of mesquite beans resonating inside the hardened gourd. My grandfather was a full-on bird singer. He could do the whole cycle, three days and nights of songs. His rattle was famous for its tone, a Stradivarius of rattles. I've had per-cap guys offer me a thousand dollars for it. I'd sooner sell my soul.

"Bird songs never lie," my grandfather would tell me on nights when we'd sing around the fire. We'd sing them over and over. Until the songs became second nature. Until they became truth. "The world can deceive, but bird songs never lie. The feeling inside when you sing is truth."

He had eyes that often focused on the distant. He gummed the songs, all his teeth yanked by BIA dentists—graying mustache, arthritic fingers, foxtails clinging to the cuffs of his jeans.

I shake my rattle, his rattle. What song should I sing? The right song arrives unbidden. I put the rasp in my voice that he taught me. A melody as old as Indian life rises from my throat, so old nobody knows what language the words come from.

I focus on Sister, nothing spiritual, just a song of consolation for what might have been. Just a song from my heart. I sing my truth.

In the distance a door slams.

"You're so full of shit. You ain't touching me with that thing!" Sister yells.

She storms toward me, kind of angry, kind of laughing in disbelief at her own stupidity. "He's no good," she says.

She nears, her eyes asking forgiveness. She kisses me on the cheek, her lips wet against my skin.

"Instagram me," she whispers, her breath warm in my ear.

She runs to her ride home.

Franklin straightens his jeans as he walks over. "Man, I was this close," he says.

I say nothing.

ABOUT THE AUTHOR

Gordon Lee Johnson, Cahuilla/Cupeño, lives and writes on the Pala Indian Reservation. A former newspaperman, he was last a columnist and feature writer for the *Press-Enterprise*, covering Southern California's Inland Empire. Prior to journalism, he studied literature and philosophy at the Universities of California at Santa Cruz, San Diego, and Berkeley.

He graduated with a degree in creative writing from Vermont College and went on to earn a master of fine arts from Antioch University, where he concentrated on Native fiction. He is currently enrolled in the Institute of American Indian Arts' MFA screenwriting program.

He has a book of newspaper columns called *Rez Dogs Eat Beans* that was translated and published in the Czech Republic. In 2007, Heyday published another compilation of his newspaper columns titled *Fast Cars and Frybread*.

He is the former Indigenous Writer in Residence for the School of Advanced Research in Santa Fe.

He has four children, eleven grandchildren, and a feral tabby cat named Trouble who growls from the back porch when hungry.

green press
INITIATIVE

Heyday is committed to preserving ancient forests and natural resources. We elected to print this title on 30% post consumer recycled paper, processed chlorine free. As a result, for this printing, we have saved:

5.4 Trees (40' tall and 6-8" diameter)
2.2 Million BTUs of Total Energy
2,300 Pounds of Greenhouse Gases
500 Gallons of Wastewater
19 Pounds of Solid Waste

Heyday made this paper choice because our printer, Thomson-Shore, Inc., is a member of Green Press Initiative, a nonprofit program dedicated to supporting authors, publishers, and suppliers in their efforts to reduce their use of fiber obtained from endangered forests.

For more information, visit www.greenpressinitiative.org

Environmental impact estimates were made using the Environmental Defense Paper Calculator. For more information visit: www.papercalculator.org.